Eleven C's for a Strong Marriage

Also by
Rodney and Cheryl
Sanderson-Smith

Eleven C's for a Strong Marriage
Workbook

Eleven C's for a Strong Marriage

Eleven Conversations for Couples

Rodney Sanderson-Smith
with
Cheryl Sanderson-Smith

Self-Published

Copyright © 2019
by Rodney and Cheryl Sanderson-Smith

All rights reserved. No part of this book may be reproduced, distributed, or transmitted in any form or by any means, including photocopying, recording, or other electronic or mechanical methods, without the prior written permission of the publisher, except in the case of brief quotations embodied in critical reviews and certain other noncommercial uses permitted by copyright law. For permission requests, write to the publisher, addressed "Attention: Permissions Coordinator," at the address below.

Rodney and Cheryl Sanderson-Smith
www.rodcherylsandersonsmith.com
www.11csforastrongmarriage.com

Ordering Information:
Quantity sales. Special discounts are available on quantity purchases by corporations, associations, and others. For details, contact the publisher at the address above.

Unless otherwise noted, Scripture quotations are from the Holy Bible, New International Version, NIV. Copyright © 1973, 1978, 1984, 2011 by Biblica, Inc.

Any internet addresses, phone numbers, or company or product information printed in this book are offered as a resource and were consistent and accurate at the time of printing and were within the values of the authors. The authors do however not vouch for the existence, content, or services of these sites, phone numbers, companies, or products beyond the day of printing.

ISBN-13: 978-0-9998185-0-3
ISBN-10: 0-9998185-0-3
Printed in the United States of America
Second Edition

14 13 12 11 10 / 10 9 8 7 6 5 4 3 2 1

*To our beautiful girls,
Tamryn, Caylin, and Emlyn
that are our consistent support
and inspiration.
We love you so very much.*

Preamble

Marriage is a JOURNEY of discovery. An adventure more exciting than you can imagine. But has to start on a solid spiritual footing. What you believe will profoundly influence your union. There will be tough times and magnificent moments. How you navigate these will develop you or destroy you.

If you are not a Christian, know that this book has not landed in your hands by chance. We pray that this moment in time will not only be the most exciting coming together of two human beings, but will also give you an opportunity to explore your spiritual understandings.

Table of Contents

Foreword
Comments. . . . . *X*

Introduction
Starting Right. *XIV*

Chapter 1
Christ
A Spiritual Conversation *2*

Chapter 2
Community and Church
A Conversation about the Family for your Family. . . .*18*

Chapter 3
Communication
A Conversation about how to Talk Right *40*

Chapter 4
Conflict
A Conversation about how to Fight Right!. *66*

Chapter 5
Common Vision
A Conversation about The Target *92*

Chapter 6
Captain
A Conversation about Who's in Charge? *114*

Chapter 7
    Clan
        A Conversation about the Tree you Marry. *134*

Chapter 8
    Career/Children
        A Conversation about the Rat Race and Rugrats! . . . *158*

Chapter 9
    Cash
        A Conversation about Bringing Home the Bacon . . . *178*

Chapter 10
    Cuddles
        A Conversation about Sex and Stuff. *198*

Chapter 11
    Celebration
        A Conversation about Faith and Fun *224*

Chapter 12
    Conclusion
        Now What? *236*

Chapter 13
    Contributions
        Bibliography. *246*

Chapter 14
    Acknowledgements
        Contributing Community. *261*

FOREWORD

Comments

Foreword

Comments

Deon Engelke

Deon is a former journalist and media manager. Today he is a director in a marketing communications company[1] based in South Africa. He has been married to Gail, a teacher, for more than twenty years. They have two beautiful daughters, both of whom are college students.

Having been married for more than twenty years, it amazes me how happy I am in marriage considering how little I knew about relationships! More amazing is how much I, as a veteran, learned from this book. I wish I had the maturity as a twenty-two year old groom to engage deeply with my partner, ahead of our marriage through insightful, frank and entertaining material like this.

This book and the incredible discussion opportunity it presents is essential for couples and deeply enriching.

Marriage preparation should never be a "crash course" or a necessary evil like it was for me and for those wanting to marry at our church, where "prep" was compulsory. This book can open the floodgates of true love in a relationship and develop an understanding of practical issues that are the source of significant pain for many married and divorced couples today.

FOREWORD

While our story has a very happy middle and, with God's help, a very happy ending, the beginning was intensely dark and hopeless. My girlfriend (now wife) became pregnant and both of us felt at the time that our lives had ended. The shame and guilt were such that suicide was contemplated. With the love of God, shown through His people, including the then youth pastor and his wife at our church (the authors of this book), our story has become part of His story of grace, love, and generosity.

INTRODUCTION

Starting Right

This book is all about preparing you for a lifelong relationship that is mutually rewarding, less puzzling and one that you would never want to exit.

Introduction

Starting Right

Comedian Bill Murray was rumored to have tweeted the following:

"Marriage is like the IKEA of relationships. Easy to walk into, confusing to piece together and difficult to exit."

This book is all about preparing you for a lifelong relationship that is mutually rewarding, less puzzling and one that you would never want to exit. It is written in plain English with practical help and information.

We sometimes cook together, from scratch. No boxes. No instants. No ordering takeout. We spend time and are purposeful about purchasing the correct ingredients and, working together, to make something delicious. Following a tried and tested recipe, we can then relax and trust that we will soon enjoy some good home-cooked food and conversation. We put the effort in, and we are very specific about the ingredients we place into the mix. The reason we do not trade salt for sugar, or lard for butter, or ground beef for ground coffee is because we want to enjoy the treat as a tasty and rewarding meal, not a repugnant, disappointing flop. There are some dangerous times when Cheryl gets creative, but let's not mention that. The higher quality the elements, the better the result.

Unfortunately, most people put less effort and prep-

INTRODUCTION

aration into their marriage than preparing the average dish from scratch, the correct way, according to the recipe book. Quite predictably, what you put in is what you get out!

If you invest in a relationship, observing what you are putting in, putting in only that which will make it form into a sweet, rewarding, satisfying experience, you will enjoy a very nourishing relationship, you will finish each other's sentences and, well if you like me, food.

> Like cooking, what you put in is what you get out!

On the flip side, there is a vast horde of salty, cynical, lonely, self-consumed old people sitting in senior centers or homes, because they placed all the wrong ingredients into the mix.

There is a nourishing recipe. We call it the
Eleven C's for a Strong Marriage.

Rod's Story: Talking of essential ingredients, to celebrate a special occasion, we were having dinner at a fancy French restaurant. You know, one of those where you cannot pronounce the items on the menu. After a wonderful main course, that could have easily been featured on the Master Chef kitchen TV show, they brought out the dessert. It was a peach cobbler or peach crisp, as some call it. The smell of warm peach and toasted oats floated through the air. Can you smell it? Not being the shy type, I made a beeline for the table and loaded up. I grabbed my spoon and dug deeply into the succulent sweet treat placing an oversized portion in my mouth. Almost on cue, someone began talking to me! To my utter disbelief, amidst cobbler and conversation all I could taste was a shockingly disgusting strong taste of *salt*! My face, most likely, resembled a deep sea fisherman squinting into a strong south west gale trying to navigate his ship home.

Being in a French restaurant, I was not sure if this was some unique form of dessert. I did not want to share my ignorance or uneducated palate with our table of guests. I hesitantly shared with the group, eager for my feedback, that it had in fact a "little ocean feel," to it.

Just as I scraped off the last morsel of peach, the rotund and blushing maitre'd scurried around collecting all the plates and informed us, with a profuse apology, that the chef had, in error, traded powdered salt for powder sugar. A replacement treat was being prepared.

The result of putting the wrong ingredient into the mix can be disastrous for desserts and marriages. The *'Eleven C's for a Strong Marriage'* is part of that excellent and correct ingredient list.

> **The result of putting the wrong ingredients into the mix can be disastrous for dishes and marriages.**

We do want to commend you for preparing for your marriage and taking the time to invest in your most important relationships. We want to encourage you to bring your partner into this preparation and engage with them in honest and open conversation. The alignment of your dreams and expectations is essential for a sweet and tasty union.

Some bad ingredients come from the past. They drag along from behind and affect the mix, sometimes unbeknownst to us.

Fueled by pornography when I was growing up, marriage seemed like a dessert to me: all to be enjoyed for my own pleasure. Like the restaurant incident, I was going to have this pleasure in copious heaps.

INTRODUCTION

When I met my wife-to-be, I thought that marriage was just a fulfillment of *my* every need and desire. I was shattered when I discovered it was a lot more than a license to have 'relations.' I had developed a distorted view of love, intimacy, and sex and brought that into our marriage.

On a side note, we will talk more about sex later in the book. Hang in there guys.

David Boehi, in his book Preparing for Marriage: Discover God's Plan for a Lifetime of Love says: "Too many couples enter marriage blinded by unrealistic expectations. They believe the relationship should be characterized by a high level of continuous romantic love. As one young adult said, 'I wanted marriage to fulfill all my desires. I needed security, someone to take care of me, intellectual stimulation, economic security immediately—but it just wasn't like that!' People are looking for something 'magical' to happen in marriage. But magic doesn't make a marriage work: hard work does."

> "Magic doesn't make a marriage work: *hard* work does."

What are your expectations of marriage?

Pictionary[1], is a game where a person has to draw an image, without using words or gestures, to describe a word written on a card. Their partner has to guess. In the same way, the picture you have of marriage may not match the picture your spouse has. We enter into marriage with presuppositions and perceptions that you have formed based on a lifetime of experiences, good and bad.

This book is designed to help you and your partner draw out your understanding of this powerful gift and lifestyle called marriage. Here, fruitful dialogue and mutual understanding sets you up for victorious living. This mutually rewarding married life tastes sweet, not salty. In essence, the Eleven C's are eleven *conversations* that would have helped Cheryl and I enter into our union better prepared. Enjoy this buffet of interaction.

> **We enter into marriage with presuppositions and perceptions that you have formed based on a lifetime of experiences, good and bad.**

The book is structured in a few ways to make it interactive and 'man' friendly. Each page has a box highlighting the most salient fact or facts from that page. Skim readers can focus on those. At the end of each chapter, we have summarized the content in ten statements or less. This is another resource, to help out our busy reading colleagues. Each chapter has an 'Action Steps' section to create movement and help facilitate understanding and communication. We have also identified stories and actions that illustrate the concepts. A quick reader can glance over the material, using our time saving tools, or the happy sojourner can delve into the entire fun and fancy of the journey.

INTRODUCTION

Speed Notes on Introduction (in ten phrases or less)

- Marriage is like cooking, what you put in is what you get out.
- Rich and rewarding relationships are the result of purposeful and significant investments in time and resources.
- People enter marriage with expectations and desires.
- Conversation is a way to unlock the heart and desires of the other person.
- We all enter into marriage with a lot of backstory influence. Our history shapes our future.
- Have you ever played Pictionary? Have you tried to describe something that you can see so clearly but the other person does not?
- Eleven C's for a Strong Marriage is a book designed to facilitate eleven important conversations to begin some great 'self' and 'other' discovery.
- This book is man-friendly and designed for speed readers.
- There are summaries and action steps for each chapter.
- Enjoy.

Action Steps

- Bake or make a tasty treat with each other. Get messy, have fun, make it from scratch. Talk about some of the things that you would like to see in your marriage as you sift, saute' and steam your way to a tasty

meal.
- Schedule eleven dates for eleven crucial conversations.
- Write a love letter to each other, but do not show it to each other. Write out the reasons why you asked her to marry you and write out the reasons you said yes. Put in the letter some of your dreams and desires, as a couple.
- Look for another couple in your same life phase and gather for an evening meal and conversation about both of your adventures into married life.

CHAPTER 1

Christ

Marriage is an immovable change of status of each person. You change from being individuals to one. God planned it that way so that you would never have to fear being torn apart or abandoned.

Chapter 1

Christ

A Spiritual Conversation

Proverbs 18:22 says

> "He who finds a wife, finds what is good and receives favor from the Lord."

Rod's Story: She took my breath away. I know all love stories have this element, but I can genuinely say that I am not sure if it was the small white reflections dancing off the mirror ball, or the colored lights moving across her dress. Perhaps it was the glass blue translucence of her eyes or maybe her dark contrasting hair bouncing to the beat. Her olive skin and perfect white teeth were mesmerizing. I watched her dance and move to the current tunes. I was immediately in love. I remember turning to my brother Michael and yelling into his ear against the pulsating music of the DJ's selection "That is a girl you marry and not one you just mess around with!"

> "That is a girl you marry and not one you just mess around with."

The following day I began the process of tracking down the owner of the glass slipper. It took some time because I had to use old-fashioned methods like talking to friends of friends of friends. Eventually, I found out she attended a local Christian youth group.

A few months later I 'happened' to arrive at her church. We hung out all night and to be honest, did not pay much attention to the Bible study. I think I remember the youth pastor speaking louder and louder, it could have been about dating or lust, but I am not sure. I know there was shouting, sweating and pounding of the Bible, so it must have been a challenging message.

I was not looking for a Christian girl. The whole Jesus thing tended to get in the way of my advances. You see, I had grown up in a very religious family. We attended church each Sunday, and I was afraid of God. He was big, grand and non-personal. But the neat part about that non-personal God is that as long as you confess, you are all set, right? So life was just about doing whatever you wanted and begging for forgiveness on the weekends. Sometimes I even went so far as to desire difficult chores and self-imposed 'punishment.' This was an attempt to convince God to forgive me, or more correctly to persuade God to erase the consequences of my stupidity. Have you ever been there?

> **I was afraid of God. He was big and grand and non-personal.**

Cheryl, on the other hand, had a very different view of God, conceived from an impacting conversation with her cousin and best friend, Linda.

Cheryl's Story: As a young child, I attended Sunday school with our extended family. One summer, we were out in the backyard enjoying the suns rays and beautiful weather when Linda, my cousin, asked me if I was a Christian. She then doubled down and followed up with, 'Are you going to heaven?' I was unsure. In true 10-year-old evangelism style, she said that if I didn't pray this prayer, then something bad would happen to me, to quote, 'You will die and go to hell!' Can you see her little

> **"Are you going to heaven?"**

finger pointing, the other hand firmly on her hip? Needless to say, we knelt in our small blue splash pool, surrounded by grass, insects and a few floaties and prayed 'the prayer.' I think an instant baptism was discussed, but we postponed that plan.

Although I was in 4th grade and only 9 years old, I felt a peace. God's love filled me, and from that moment I desired to grow and learn more about God. I got a Bible for Christmas that year. I remember praying earnestly to God about everything and feeling as though He was right next to me. On a side note, I remember my aunt telling me I was going to marry a pastor.

Clearly we began our relationship from different spiritual understandings. I started from a religious mindset where confession and consequence were paramount, and Cheryl approached from a relationship paradigm where intimacy and instruction held the high ground. These contrasting launch points caused us to relate to spiritual things from opposite poles. My direction and hers were almost contradictory. My behaviors had nothing to do with my spirituality while, for Cheryl, her actions showed everything about her spirituality. She even dragged me to a Vacation Bible School, where amongst screaming kids and messy playdough, God began spiritual formation in me. You do anything when you are in love, right? However we were certainly still not heading in the same destination. I even tried to get her to leave youth group one night to head to a party, she declined. We soon parted ways.

It took a bullet, a boy and a bad day for me (Rod) to take a relationship with

> **Christ or spiritual formation is the first topic we will discuss because it affects everything.**

God seriously. But more about that later.

Christ or spiritual formation is the first topic we will discuss because it affects everything. It sets our launch point, our movement, our direction, our landing, our propulsion, our construct, and our contexts. It is not something that you can easily place to the side and ignore. It is the cornerstone of life.

The Designer

As you begin this discovery of your relationship or marital journey, have you thought about exploring the God who designed it? We only noticed the versatility of our smartphones after seeing a post on social media. These tutorials highlighted the amazing untapped potential by exposing the many unknown features. There are striking similarities to our relationship with God and our understanding of marriage. There are many surprising, deeper aspects you could discover and enjoy if you are faithful and reflective through the pages of this book.

Some of the tools written about in this book can be used immediately, with instant results. Others will take a lifetime to master. But all are available to everyone, and all of them come from our discovery of God and His heart for His creation of marriage. Genesis 2:18:

> *'The LORD God said, "It is not good for the man to be alone. I will make a helper suitable for him."*

The Design

We believe that marriage is God's idea. He is the Architect, the mastermind, so it would make sense to embody His perspective. This was not always my view, but

> **God designed marriage, embody His perspective.**

the more we entered into the conversation, the more we discovered God's masterplan. We pray this book will do some of that for you too.

In Genesis, the first book of the Bible, we find that God created the first human. This man, Adam, is then commissioned to name all the animals. Did you notice that? Remember that names meant something back then. Fathers would name their children based on characteristics they saw in their offspring. Sometimes a name would be something they affirm. Sometimes a prayer or prophecy for them. There are some cultures that, still today, will wait to name their babies. It could take a few weeks or more before they can identify some of 'who' their child is.

Adam was calling out and noticing the traits and characteristics of the animals, naming them, and giving them each a title. He was seeing things that made them unique and intentionally created. God brings them all past him. Adam calls out their characters but sees nothing that resonated with the completeness of his own personal revelation. Although they were all fantastic, there was an incompleteness in each of them.

> **The first man Adam was needing something that resonated with his heart.**

Sort of like if you are standing at the airport waiting for a family member to appear from a long trip away. People arrive and others respond. Some have signs, and some have tears. But nothing moves you quite like when you see your loved ones silhouette behind the opaque glass. Is it them? Could it be? Notice the walk, the characteristics, and then before you know it, there are hugs, hollers and hallelujahs! Everyone else in the concourse melts away. Your eyes block out all the unfamiliar people, noises and images. Your emotions respond, your heart jumps.

God knows that. I speculate God was showing Adam

all there was and Adam was looking for someone who resonated with him and made his heart skip a beat. He is left celebrating God's creativeness but saddened by creation's lack of connection with him, as a human.

God notices that His most valued creation is still lonely. The man has observed the interaction and unity of all the animals in the garden. He has seen the moose and the goose with their equal love partners. He has seen the bat and the rat and named them, in the end, there was nothing that reflected him or drew him. God notices this and says, 'It is not good for man to be alone.' (Genesis 2:18) God said that man was created in His image; he is a gendered image bearer.

The man needed a perfect community; he needed another human, and he needed the Holy presence of God. God knows this because He, himself, exists in a continuous triune perfect relationship. God exists in the community of the Trinity (the Father, Son, and Holy Spirit). So God created a woman. These people, the Bible says, are formed in His image (Genesis 1:27[1]).

In the community of God, there is no tension, nothing lacking and no disharmony because each member devotes themselves to the other. That is it.

The vision God created for humankind is in the commitment and enlightenment of a marriage relationship.

God created us to share in the harmony and perfect love of His community where relationships are selfless, secure and always affirming of the other.

John Joseph Powell in The Secret of Staying in Love says,

> **Marriage is designed to reflect the community of God.**

"It is an absolute human certainty that no one can know his own beauty or perceive a sense of his own worth until it has been reflected back to him in the mirror of another loving, caring human being."

In the loving community of the Trinity, interdependence is only surpassed by love, appreciation, and affirmation.

The Designer chose for us to be within a united male and female couple to procreate. This secure and thriving selfless community is needed to further humanity so the next generation can get a glimpse of Him, and His selfless love.

Some creatures can self-procreate, like some jellyfish, sea anemones, and flatworms. There are even some greenflies, stick insects, aphids, water fleas, scorpions, termites and honey bees that can multiply without fertilization. Most could not get a date anyway, but humanity needs each other. We are dependent on both genders for the very survival of our species.

Why is this important? It highlights the need we have for each other, for relationships. We were never designed to navigate this globe on our own. You will always feel the need for community, it is deep within you. Why do you think people make such bad connecting decisions? Why do you think people 'hook up' carelessly? Whether online or in the bar, they know the next day they will feel used or like a user? The 'walk of shame' is not just an ethnic slogan but an emotional and relational reality.

> God chose for us to be within a secure, selfless community to procreate and thrive so the next generation can get a glimpse, of Him, and His selfless love.

If this were not God's perfect plan (and if He did not exist), we would merely have evolved towards self-procreation and self-gratification. Marriage is beautiful and wonderful, but it is also very tough. Just think of your anxiety and tensions the first time you asked her/him for a date? It is much easier to migrate into one's selfish cocoon than to venture out and risk building lifelong relationships. Our earthly relationships help us grow as individuals, and in that personal struggle, we develop our dependence on God, drawing us closer to Him.

Against this backdrop, we see God unpacking marriage. There is never a consideration by the triune God, of separation or disintegration. That is why the Biblical language used, is so strong. Look at Matthew 19: 4-6:

> *"Haven't you read," he replied, "that at the beginning the Creator 'made them male and female,' and said, 'For this reason a man will leave his father and mother and be united to his wife, and the two will become one flesh'? So they are no longer two, but one flesh. Therefore what God has joined together, let no one separate."*

You become one flesh. Only the couples that make it to their silver years can really help us understand this.

Rod's Story: I visited a senior center as part of my hospice job. I got to observe a small, jovial, rotund man caring for his ageing wife. She had survived a devastating stroke. He would sometimes stir at 3 am, missing his bride. He would

> In marriage, you become one flesh. Only the couples that make it to their silver years and have been married for many anniversaries can really help us understand and see this.

jump in his car and head to her to just sit in the dark at the foot of her bed watching her breath in and out until she awoke. And when she did rise, this beautiful southern raised gospel girl would uncharacteristically let out a tirade of vulgar expletives about everything from the nursing care to his stupidity for not fixing her health problems. Her personality had changed, and she had become combative and cantankerous. She would moan at him and make unreasonable demands of staff, and of his time and attention. Before she even asked or needed something he was already moving towards her to complete the task. All the while his love and compassion for her were evident in all the ways he tirelessly cared for her. He would lean over and say to me, 'That's not her you know, it is the sickness speaking." His love for her was unwavering through these difficult times, 'through sickness and in health', right?

This is God's picture, a commitment, a covenant, someone taking his/her vows seriously and loving even when it's hard. They are a couple who understood when something is broken you fix it, you do not get rid of it. That is a couple who have become one flesh.

The wedding vow and the commitment you are about to make to each other is not some trite ditty to bring an 'ooh' or 'ah' from the audience. It is a pledge and covenant to each other. It is more than a promise, it is life-long learning. The more we began to understand the meaning, value and dedication of marriage, the more secure we felt in it. We understand that we are emulating the Godhead and making a covenant before each other and God. It is

> **Marriage is not a decision of convenience with the bonus of free sex. It is a new way of life designed by God.**

CHRIST

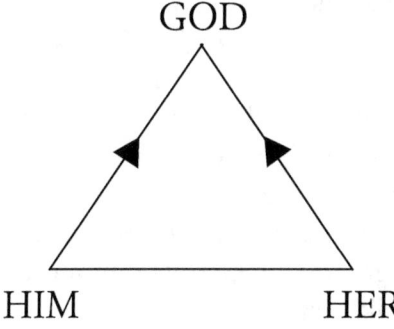

Figure 1

different. It is not a shallow hope grown out of young love that promises only daisies and rainbows. It is not a decision of convenience with the bonus of free sex. It is a new way of life designed by God.

Now the best way to understand this covenant and commitment is to see God's understanding through Scripture. Genesis 2: 21-24:

> "So the Lord God caused the man to fall into a deep sleep; and while he was sleeping, he took one of the man's ribs and then closed up the place with flesh. Then the Lord God made a woman from the rib he had taken out of the man, and he brought her to the man. The man said, "This is now bone of my bones and flesh of my flesh; she shall be called 'woman,' for she was taken out of man." That is why a man leaves his father and mother and is united to his wife, and they become one flesh."

It is an immoveable change of status of each person. You change from being individuals to one. God planned it that way so that you would never have to fear being torn apart or abandoned.

Here we see a bride and groom standing before God, the Witness, as they promise and pledge themselves to each

11

other in permanence. That's why it's not taken lightly. *It is an immovable change of status of each person.* You change from being individuals to one 'flesh.' This covenant is understood through the lens of God's promises to Adam and then humanity as a whole. God did the work and made the way. It is a commitment and cost that He carried. This is the same designed structure for marriage. A man and a woman are united through God by God who never fails, never leaves and never walks away.

God planned it that way so that you would never have to fear being torn apart or abandoned. You are never supposed to be ripped into pieces like a bullet destroying flesh. You are supposed to enjoy edifying love in this safe community. This community now moves towards Christlikeness. This reality gives it a focus and culture. Think of it as a triangle with a man and a woman at two corners and Christ at the third. (Refer to Figure 1) The closer the man and the woman get to Christ, the closer they get to each other.

When both husband and wife are purposeful about learning to live life more and more like Jesus, the natural result is that you get closer and closer to each other. You are both heading to the same point of the arrow, the same destination, selfless community, pure love!

The converse, couples that head in their own and different directions. Imagine if you begin at a train station in Chicago and one person is heading east to New York and the other west to San Francisco. Through time you get further and further apart. The harder you 'try,' the faster and further you separate from each other.

This all begins with a commitment to Jesus and His way.

> **This all begins with a commitment to Jesus.**

Rod's Story: I remember getting the 'Dear John,' letter while in the army. I was devastated. My greatest fear became a reality, my Christian girlfriend had become refocused on God. His will and His way. She had been going to the Green House Bible study and was challenged about whether God really was her primary priority. She realized I was not heading in the same direction. She broke it off. Something about being 'unequally yoked' (2 Corinthians 6:14), I don't know! I confess there was begging, crying, manipulative talk, bribery, coercion, but she stayed the course.

This common destination sets the course. You are establishing the platform to have an intimacy and a closeness that is Divine. You are preparing to share in a calling, vision, and life that only those seasoned followers of Jesus understand and can articulate. When your attitude to marriage is aligned with Jesus, you are gentle, forgiving, patient, selfless and sacrificial. Essentially this means you put your spouses needs over your own, you serve them.

When only one partner exercises this committed relating there are benefits, but with a higher risk for hurts and abuse. When both partners act in this God-directed way, then you are living life abundantly and as God created life to be lived! This facilitates a real meaningful connection. Notice the enjoyment and richness captured in the lines of Scripture. Proverbs 5:18:

> **When you act in this God-directed way, then you are really living.**

'May your fountain be blessed, and may you rejoice in the wife of your youth.'

However, this is only enjoyed in the context of a relationship with God. Do you have one? Are you living your life in such a way that you are becoming more Christ-like each day? That would mean that you have decided to make what is called a commitment to become a Christ follower. He becomes the CEO of your life and calls the shots. His will and His way become your roadmap and marching orders. Have you, like Cheryl, had a 'knelt down in a small blue splash pool' moment? Can you remember a time when you said yes to Jesus? Have you experienced the peace that comes from a fully surrendered faith in God?

Action: Have your first conversation with each other about your spiritual understandings and unpack your belief structure. This is the first and most important conversation you will have. This is the first C - Christ. For some of you this will be the first time you have considered it, but take a look at what a famous author C.S. Lewis says in his book Mere Christianity:

> **Have your first conversation with each other about your spiritual beliefs.**

"I am trying here to prevent anyone saying the really foolish thing that people often say about Him: I'm ready to accept Jesus as a great moral teacher, but I don't accept his claim to be God. That is the one thing we must not say. A man who was merely a man and said the sort of things Jesus said would not be a great moral teacher. He would either be a lunatic — on the level with the man who says he is a poached egg — or else he would be the Devil of Hell. You must

> **Jesus was a lunatic or the Savior of the world. You get to choose. This is your moment. It will change everything!**

make your choice. Either this man was, and is, the Son of God, or else a madman or something worse. You can shut him up for a fool, you can spit at him and kill him as a demon or you can fall at his feet and call him Lord and God, but let us not come with any patronizing nonsense about his being a great human teacher. He has not left that open to us. He did not intend to."

What C.S. Lewis makes clear is that we do not have many options when it comes to responding to the historical Jesus. He walked on earth and made audacious claims that demand a response. The testimony of his life was so impacting, the integrity of His witness and words were so life transforming that His disciples were prepared to commit their lives to serve His cause. He chose a brutal death on the cross by claiming His divine nature. He was a lunatic or the Savior of the world. You get to choose, but you cannot ignore the question. This is your moment. You get to make the evaluation and decision right now, and it will change everything!

You have no option but to head straight into the question. We are calling men to be loving, gentle but firm in this matter.

Action: Men, this is the time to lean in and ask your spouse, girlfriend or bride. What do you believe?

You have to make a decision. You can say:

- I need more time to consider faith in Jesus.

> We have to respond to the historical Jesus. His life and death force a reaction.

- I would *not* like to 'go to hell,' I would like a 'small blue splash pool' moment, I would like to become a Christian, now.
- I believe in Jesus, and my life needs to more accurately reflect that.
- I am passionate for Jesus, my life does reveal that, and I would like us to journey towards Christlikeness together, and encourage others.

If this is your first time, a refocus or recommitment, find a way to commemorate this moment. How about writing your name and date on a Christmas ornament? Now each year at that special time of the season, you are reminded of today and can celebrate all over again.

ABCD
Accept Jesus
Believe in His sacrifice for me
Commit my life to Him
Dedicate myself to loving others.
A simple but profound roadmap to faith in Christ.

Speed Notes on Chapter 1

- Spiritual conversations are vitally important; it changes everything.
- What are your spiritual stories?
- What are your spiritual directions?
- Are you and your spouse heading in the same direction?
- God designed marriage.
- One man needs one woman, and one woman needs one man. It's not complicated. It's profound, and this, and only this, most completely represents God.
- We are designed in a relationship, for a relationship, you relate?
- You become one flesh.
- It all begins with Jesus Christ.
- You cannot ignore Jesus Christ, His life and statements do not allow for that.

Action Steps

- Have a date and enter gently into the spiritual or Christ conversation.
- Engage seriously in exploration of Christianity from a relational, not religious, perspective.
- Be honest with yourself. What is your spiritual story? What is your theological world view? How are you going to become who you want to be?
- Find someone you trust, possibly a close Christian friend or pastor, and have an honest spiritual conversation with them.
- Engage in the spiritual disciplines of Study and Journaling.

ELEVEN C'S FOR A STRONG MARRIAGE

CHAPTER 2

Community and Church

These smaller gatherings within a church, or part of a wider body of churches, are the most effective incubators for life change.

Chapter 2

Community and Church

A Conversation about the Family for your Family

The second key ingredient to a great marriage or the second "C" is the role of Community and Church in your life.

The great American evangelist Dwight L. Moody is quoted as saying: "Church attendance is as vital to a disciple as a transfusion of rich, healthy blood to a sick man," while music superstar Justin Bieber is reputed to say: "You don't need to go to church to be a Christian. If you go to Taco Bell, that doesn't make you a taco." Homer Simpson has an even more extreme view of the church: "I'm having the best day of my life, and I owe it all to not going to Church!"

> "Church attendance is as vital to a disciple as a transfusion of rich, healthy blood to a sick man"

Whether you lean towards Moody, Bieber or Simpson's perspective, it is accepted that church is a unique place. Most are a place of community, companionship, accountability, reverence, reflection, spirituality, teaching, training, helping and more. Church, from a biblical perspective, is a gathering or assembly of people with the goal of learning, understanding and growing in their faith. This can be experienced in environments ranging from a small group to a mega-gathering.

Rod's Story: Church had stolen my girl! I was now

alone at an army base and dumped. You know, the hard kind. The kind that leaves you devastated, shocked, hurt and confused. I was angry with the Church. I was mad with the Green House Bible study group that had convinced and coerced my girl away from me. I hated Charles the leader. I decided to hike down to get my girl, armed with my military issue nine millimeter handgun and a bad attitude to match.

I immediately jumped on the road and hiked down to my home town. At times it took a minute or sometimes hours to catch a ride, so you grabbed what you could. This time a trucker pulled over. These are always interesting moments because you do not know who this is, how they drive or in fact anything about them. Just that they are heading in the same direction as you want to go. So picture this, burley trucker guy, traveling through the night, a mad soldier dozing in the passenger seat. Now I began dreaming, and in my dream, I imagined the driver dozing off. I saw the truck begin to drift across lanes and next thing I awoke in a panic and slapped Mr Trucker and yelled 'Wake Up!!' He was as shocked as I was. We both looked at each other for an awkward minute, as I tried to explain my erratic behavior, and I know what he was thinking, 'What strange character did I pick up?'

I got to my home town and 'surprised' Cheryl at her Bible study group. It was strange to me, different, perplexing. They were circled up and were singing. Something was different, something was tangible. My anger was quickly syphoned off, my rage turned to curiosity, my attitude to attention. Charles spoke, people worshiped, Cheryl prayed. God was there. This small group seemed to care genuinely for each other, and even for me! I did not

> Something was different, something was tangible. God was there.

know how to respond. I left to go back to base feeling like I had really met God but not sure what to do with that. This was unfamiliar to me. It would take a bullet and an Emergency Room for me to decide to become a Christian, but more about that later.

The Church is simply a group of people on a change continuum. Unfortunately, these very same people, create a chance for hurt, misunderstanding, confusion, and conflict. These 'drawbacks' should not cause us to 'throw the baby out with the bathwater' because the Christian church and Christian community are the very vehicles Jesus most commonly uses to present Himself and facilitate life transformation in individuals and families.

Church was a cornerstone for us. It was where we met, where we grew in faith, experienced God, learned about missions, discovered God's voice, and found a solid Christian community.

The church includes many valuable attributes. We will look at two: *Divinity and Community*.

Divinity

God says we should worship him. There is a reason. It is not because He is some self-consumed pompous God that needs us minions to run around and praise Him. He does not need us to make Him feel significant or valued. He does, however, know that worship is in our design. He has placed the capacity and passion for worship, and the perfect fit for us, is to worship Him[1]. The great added blessing is that He always pours back into us!

> **Worship God, you can never outgive Him. Go ahead and try!**

That's right, you can never out-give God. So, the more you worship, the more complete (fuller) you become, if your agenda is correct, of course. Everybody is hard-wired to worship so all people will aspire to worship something, all the time. It is a pull.

Action: Think of some examples of things people worship.

Our human desire to worship manifests as obsessions and addictions. Some examples of things we worship are girls, boys, money, cars, careers, popularity, fitness and just about anything you can think of. What consumes your thoughts, time and money? You will find many people exhausted and disillusioned at the foot of many of these self-built effigies. You will see many giving of themselves to idols that give nothing back. God's request to worship Him is His way of saving us from ourselves.

God literally says, 'Worship Me, because I love you and will pour back into you. Worshipping something else will exasperate and erode you. Let Me help you, by calling you, to worship Me.'

I had a new and fresh understanding of God! I was now passionate about getting involved in church, and fully embraced the roller coaster of small group community. Faith based activities were no longer a chore. We began attending weekly community worship services. This faithful habit created the focused time to reflect, ponder and exalt God. We also began daily habits of personal prayer, Bible reading, and devotions. But God does something unique in the presence of His gathered people.

> Going regularly to church is a faithful habit that will create the focused time to reflect, ponder and exalt God.

Here our worship of God is unpacked in the form of loving actions. We used our gifts to worship God, and for Gods' witness. Here we hear messages that we have not chosen so God can reveal to us areas He wants to illuminate.

We have a tendency to slant and skew our learning to satisfy our desire to validate our current perspective. This leans towards absorbing information from our reading, observing and listening with rose-colored glasses or filters. We then draw out of our 'teaching' only what we want to hear. This isolated assimilation of content has the unfortunate result of often vaccinating individuals against the very message they are exploring.

We realized that we could not be solo Christians. Staying out of a community of believers, is like a burning coal that sits outside the fire. It is only a matter of time the cold lure of society will suck the very heat out of your soul. By the way, you will not notice until it is too late.

> You cannot be a solo Christian.

The flip side, when you choose to, perhaps, do what Justin Bieber was alluding to (staying away from church) the church walks with a limp. Because a piece of it is missing, possibly sitting in some hunting stand.

Action: Take a few moments to have a conversation with your spouse about your thoughts and feelings of a local Christian church. What have been some of your experiences? What do you think the local church is there for? Who or what do you actually worship? Look up these scriptures and ponder them with one another.

Luke 4 verse 8:

Jesus answered, "It is written: 'Worship the Lord your

God and serve him only.'''

Exodus 20 verse 3 and 4:

'You shall have no other gods before me. You shall not make for yourself an image in the form of anything in heaven above or on the earth beneath or in the waters below. You shall not bow down to them or worship them; for I, the Lord your God, am a jealous God, punishing the children for the sin of the parents to the third and fourth generation of those who hate me, but showing love to a thousand generations of those who love me and keep my commandments.'

Hebrews 10:25:

'Let us not give up meeting together, as some are in the habit of doing, but let us encourage one another--and all the more as you see the Day approaching.'

Rod's Story: My church experience was diverse. I grew up in church wearing a dress, let me qualify: I sang in the boys' choir, and yes, it was a very traditional Anglican church, and we literally dressed the part! The large building structure oozed respect. The large grey granite, the huge arch ceilings, the dramatic stained glass reaching high up into the eves, echoing the choirs vocals. Have you seen any of the royal weddings? That was some of my spiritual heritage! God's presence permeated and presented itself from the very architectural arcades. The very place demanded respect and awe for God.

> This worship place demanded respect and awe for God, worshiping here was filled with breathtaking honor.

Worshiping here was filled with breathtaking honor. I can still hear the voices of the musicians singing the 'Nunc Dimittis' and the Gregorian chants echoing from the lay minister cantatas. No matter how powerful and religious my experience, I drifted from God.

Cheryl, on the other hand, was raised in a far more contemporary environment. Here, the organ pipes were traded for guitar plectrums, the choir for the chorus, the liturgy for the lyricist and the incense for instruments. Worship was refreshing, energizing and contextual. This auditorium environment was intimate, personal and friendly. Understanding that God wanted a personal relationship was comfortable here. He felt very close. It was all about relationship, small groups taught her about how God wants to be in constant community with us.

The potential risk, unfortunately, was that God could be treated as a mere colleague or buddy, and not the Great Creator God that spoke each one of us into existence. His power we cannot even imagine. Power that should not be taken lightly.

> Worshiping in this auditorium environment was intimate, personal and friendly. Understanding that God wanted a personal relationship with me was easy here. He felt very close and very intimate.

We all need to have the passion, discipline, commitment and boldness to attend a weekly gathering of Christians whether they meet in a grand cathedral or school hall. This is our opportunity to worship God. Here God and His glory are manifest. Corporate worship can raise your spirits to the very heavens. There is nothing like the reverberating words of 'Amazing grace' sung with a full band, even including a choir, perhaps even a pipe organ! Or place yourself on the auditorium floor filled with young people at a Christian conference and listen as they lead from the floor.

One should Church shop. Take the time to visit a few different places. We suggest going about 3 times in a row before trying somewhere else. Not every Church fits every person or family. That is, find one that preaches from the Bible, and that challenges you.

Rod's Story: After each of us became refocused, God called us into mission and ministry immediately, by very clearly giving me an idea for a very much needed 4th and 5th-grade youth group at our local church. I wrote all this down in a letter to Cheryl, put a good old fashion stamp on it and placed it in the mailbox. What I did not know, at that same time, is Cheryl had a dream of a youth group with 4th and 5th graders and she was writing a letter and placing it in the mail. The letters crossed in the postal system, and we both opened a vision from God.

An amusing anecdote is that when we approached that local church leadership with the vision, their first response was to decline the dream. We asked permission to give it a shot and accept the outcome no matter how devastating it could be. We just knew God said it so we would do it! A few months and many miracles later we had a program for over 100 kids, that 'could not be done,' because God made it happen.

God is not dead! God is alive, let Him draw you in.

> **God is not dead! God is alive, let Him draw you in.**

Community

We discovered that Church creates a safe spiritual home where true community can develop. God, Himself lives in community. He enjoys the unity of the Trinity (A quick note of theology: Trinity means that God exists as one god in three persons Father, Son and Holy Spirit - this can be a touch confusing, but in essence the three persons have perfect harmony in amongst themselves thereby forming the perfect community). He enjoys community so much He wants us to experience it. That is why the very begining of life begins in community.

> "The next best thing to being wise oneself is to live in a circle of those who are."

This community, the biological family, is supposed to be a micro version of the macro broader community we enjoy with others. The local church becomes a small version or the visual representation of the Triune God and a micro version of the global church. The local church is where one can enjoy some of the resources of God, presented through the gifts, talents, and skills of the community of people.

On this score, famous Christian author CS Lewis said:

> "The next best thing to being wise oneself is to live in a circle of those who are."

Rod's Story: In my office, I have a tapestry of an African hut and on it is weaved the image of three women, one has a baby strapped to her back, the other appears pregnant and the 3rd the youngest, appears to be another child of the women in the hut. The hut is in the center of the artwork. They all appear to be in a similar life phase, so there is mutual understanding, there is wise counsel. There are some women ahead and some behind. The older women are wiser. The younger keep the others energized. The story is told that in the hut a woman is delivering her child. The others have come to care and wait on her, to love and care for her, to carry her worries and provide for her needs. They bring her water and look after her children because they love her and know that there will be a day in the future when she will help those women and others that are in need. In Africa it is said 'it takes a village to raise a child' and that is the Polaroid image captured in the woven art. We say it takes a village to do life well!

Within a safe and transparent community people can get close enough to know the real you, and for you to be known. This closeness is scary for the average person, as masks and facades are the norm in our modern culture. Here are the right resources and tools for the development of Christ-likeness in oneself.

> **In a small group, we begin to learn and develop from one another in areas of spiritual, physical, social, emotional and relational growth.**

Pastor Andy Stanley from North Point Ministries in Atlanta, Georgia said it like this: "[Life-change] happens a little bit in rows and a lotta bit in circles."

Here, rows refer to sitting in a church service. Circles refer to small groups or home groups. The Bible highlights this sentiment in Proverbs 27:17:

'As iron sharpens iron, so one person sharpens another.'

ELEVEN C'S FOR A STRONG MARRIAGE

Our Village:
The Binnings, Packers, Roots, Engelkes, Van Royens,
Daubermans (absent for this picture) and us

We all have needs and areas of potential growth. Blind spots. No matter how loving and attentive our parents are/were, we all come through life with scars and stories. These back stories become apparent when we get into close community. The masks begin to disintegrate one small story, one conversation, one question, at a time. We begin to learn and develop from one another in areas of spiritual, physical, social, emotional and relational growth. This tacit learning experience is excellent. There is often osmosis of knowledge and understanding that moves through the room and community. Everyone is a student and everyone is a teacher.

> We all have blind spots. We all come through life with perspective altering scars and stories.

Rod's Story: As a South African male, I grew up in a culture where men protected the women from lions and the women, well the women did everything else. So when it came to the nurturing of my first born daughter, this would clearly be, predominantly, my wife's 'blessing.'

One Friday night at small group, we were sitting and chatting while Cheryl was preparing dinner for the whole small group, some fifteen people. At some point my daughter, Caylin, at 3 months of age, needed a diaper change. So, of course, like any man, I assessed the situation, I calculated the risks and decided my action steps. I yelled across the house to Cheryl, 'Hey Cheryl, the kid needs a fresh diaper, it's hanging on the floor and dragging behind her behind.' My American friends were shocked! They pulled me aside and as lovingly as they could, said that they were sure that I could handle this one. I was stunned! I changed the baby!

This began a journey of discovery about caring and nurturing our children that would alter my very thoughts and perspectives. This unlocked a beautiful blessing for the children. Our small group exposed a blind spot for me and 'changed' our entire lives. I now know how to change a diaper!

Unfortunately, Westernized philosophy encourages us to think more highly of ourselves than we ought. We focus our individual efforts on self-dependence and independence. This leaves our neighbors and friends, not as the object of our love and compassion, but instead considered a competitor in some warped and distorted way. To some extent, we all have neighbors named 'The Jones', and boy do we have to keep up with them. Did you know that the Jones just signed Bobby up for an extra travel sports team? Romans 12:3 says:

> 'Do not think of yourself more highly than you ought, but rather think of yourself with sober judgment, in accordance with the measure of faith God has given you.'

In under developed countries, the value of the tribe is more important than an individual's own feelings. In South Africa, this can take a humorous turn when family members believe that because one of the family has healthcare coverage, the rest can enjoy the benefits, because after all, they are one community, so the personal healthcare card will be passed around to the next in need. Here, in an illegal, and slightly humorous way, life is seen as more valuable lived out by serving others (common good) than lived out for themselves. 1 Corinthians 12:7 says

> "Now to each one the manifestation of the Spirit is given for the common good."

We are here for one another. Satan wants to divide and conquer us. Cocooning is one of the curses of our generation. (Also kale chips, but that belongs to another conversation.)

> **Cocooning is one of the curses of our generation.**

Prolific Christian author John Ortberg in his book *Everybody's Normal Till You Get to Know Them,* shocks us with this statement: "Ever console or scold people hurt in human relationships that satisfaction comes from God alone? Stop. Adam's fellowship with God was perfect, and God Himself declared Adam needed other humans."

Small Groups

These smaller gatherings within a church or part of a more extensive body of churches, are the most effective incubators for life change. They take many forms, for example, Bible study groups, serving groups, and common interest groups. They move people towards each other, breaking down barriers and building relationships. We feel strongly about the power and effect of these groups that we would prioritize a small Christian group over going to a church service if you have to make a choice. We think the Apostle Paul had small house churches in mind when he wrote his letters that are a vital part of the Bible.

> These smaller gatherings within a Church or part of a wider body of Churches are the most effective incubators for life change.

Story: The relationships we developed in our small group grew strong and deep. Some of those people now live on the other side of the globe. After more than 20 years, any one of them, would drop everything to meet us, or any of our closest friends, with thirty seconds notice.

We can share stories of retreats, conferences, adventures, missions and many more. We have pictures together as singles, then as couples, then with small children. Our frame has had to keep expanding to encompass our growing tribe. Now we are relying on those once 'small children' to further grow the family. 'Common guys, we need some grandkids to spoil!'

Even though we hadn't seen our friend's son, Mike, since he was 8 years old, he recently spent a month in the USA with us.

On the rare occasion, when we get together, we often laugh so hard, late into the night, that our guts hurt, our eyes cry, and our cheeks ache the next day. Real community is risky, but this true community is so rich and rewarding that we hunger for more small group contexts like these everywhere God sends us.

It is here men can invest in men and women can walk with women and couples can encourage couples. Accountability is the recognition we cannot do life alone, well. In the past decade, life coaches have become fashionable in business and commerce, but the church has been doing this for years. We call them mentors or accountability partners. (Some churches use the term, men's groups, accountability groups, life groups)

> It is here that men can push on men and women can walk with women and couples can encourage couples.

Serving Groups are worth mentioning because they can include the opportunity for accountability and transparency. At the same time, these groups develop the tools to grow a servant's heart and teach you to care for others above yourself. This is a gift to a good marriage, a building block, and a key ingredient. This will till the soil to break down the calcified crust that develops over the narcissistic soul. Have you ever tried to take a cookie from a baby? Say no more!

Another great reason is when things get tough, you have a team to call on. Let's get real, life is tough. Tough stuff happens. As I write this, I am praying for a beautiful little 2-year old that got an ear infection that grew into her brain and caused three large abscesses. She is on the edge of life. I'm also counseling a man who has just lost the love of his life due to stupid mistakes. I am also counseling a couple trying to work things out, where

> When things get tough you have a team to call. Life is tough, let's get real.

the husband has been surfing porn in the late hours of the night. This is a time when a team is a welcomed relief.

It takes a team to do life. They are there to carry you when you have times of spiritual, physical, social, emotional, relational and other needs. All of us, at some time, become exhausted and depleted. This might not be you today, but there will be a day when you need a hand up, a group of others to carry the load, like in the tapestry, someone to bring you water. Right now you might be the one uplifting the others. But there will be a day when you will need to be lifted up yourself.

The Opposite

The antithesis to this is egocentrism. An egocentric philosophy ignores social causes or has little or no regard for interests, beliefs, or attitudes other than one's own. 'Psychology Today' goes on to say that there is a very fine line between egocentrism and narcissism (extreme selfishness, with a grandiose view of one's own talents and a craving for admiration, as characterizing a personality type[2]). Satan loves to use this wedge to separate humankind from each other. If we can all cocoon and love ourselves to the extreme, we will not be lovers of God and lovers of others as God commands in Romans 13:9:

> *The commandments, "You shall not commit adultery," "You shall not murder," "You shall not steal," "You shall not covet," and whatever other command there may be, are summed up in this one command: "Love your neighbor as yourself."*

> **If we all cocoon and love ourselves we will not be lovers of God and lovers of others.**

There are too many things to know, too many things to navigate, too many questions unanswered to tackle married life in isolation. It might seem romantic to head to a desert island and eat bananas and make love. But honestly, that is not God's design and not his will for your life. God's design for us is to be in community and embody His very presence. Here on earth, we have the opportunity to exude the very essence of His resonance and personality. Dive into an excellent Christian community where you can give and receive. Here you will be inspired to change the world, one relationship at a time.

Cheryl's Story: Myself, our daughter and our new baby arrived in Manchester, UK. It was a typically overcast, rainy and misty British day. We were excited for the forthcoming mission. We were trying 'family style' mission and gathering with hundreds of people from all over the world to do an outreach to the local community. Housing was a temporary tent village in the central park. It was not long before the rugby ball (football) was out and we had an enjoyable game going. About 15 minutes into the fun, a dart and weave move turned into a snap and pop. Rod went down hard and grabbed his ankle. He appeared in terrible pain. My daughter held her poncho above his face to keep the rain off, as he tried to hold back tears. Imagine thousands of students from around the world, all setting up tents for living quarters and him lying on his back trying to get medical assistance. Our team carried Rod and all our belongings to base camp. These were fully loaded backpacks with tons of kid and baby supplies. Looking alot like a pack horse on an Indiana Jones quest, some ended up carrying four or more backpacks!

We are not going to mention the bottle of breast milk that burst and ran all down the backpack of our fearless leader Mark. We smelled him way before we saw him for the rest of the mission.

After an assessment and xray, the on site doctor instructed Rod to exercise and massage the ankle. Being an overachiever, he tried to rotate and work his ankle multiple times each day. With strange grinding noises and sharp

COMMUNITY AND CHURCH

pains, he continued until it expanded to the size of a soccer ball. I am not a doctor, but I thought that something possibly might just not be right. Back in the States, they diagnosed the ankle was indeed broken and placed it in a cast.

Amidst chaos we learned what a team was, and what bad medical looks like! It took a whole team! A team to move our gear, a team to care for us, a team to cover our chores, a team to move us back over the ocean, a team we will never forget.

There are times when, no matter how independent, no matter how competent, no matter how organized, no matter how planned life is, you need others! We all need Community!

Speed Notes on Chapter 2

- Christian community and church are vitally important.
- The Church has many attributes, two of them are: Divinity and Community.
- God says we should worship Him because everyone is hardwired to worship something.
- Church and small groups are for you, and are for others (through you).
- Christian community is a time to learn, listen, contribute, grow, encourage, impact, care, challenge, commiserate, study, sit back, and more.
- Small groups are a reflection of God's existential community.
- Small groups allow you to drop your masks and nuke your fears. A place for when life gets tough, and unfortunately, it will.
- Real change happens in small groups, not in church pews or rows.
- Some small groups get you involved in activities that grow your outward-looking skills. Remember 'it's not about you!'.
- Egocentric narcissism is the opposite of love. It is a self-consuming disease that attacks all of us.

Action Steps

- Have a date and enter gently into a small group and church conversation.
- Engage seriously in an exploration of Chris-

COMMUNITY AND CHURCH

tian groups and churches in your area
- It will take three visits anywhere to really 'check it out', the first time all is new and scary, the second time you do not get lost, the third time you are actually paying attention and might even recognize someone. Now you can make an informed decision to remain or not.
- Shop for a spiritual home. Shop as you did for a house. It's not easy and can take some folk more than a year and include some travel to find the Christian family for your family.
- Exercise the spiritual discipline of *Guidance and Confession* by engaging in Christian Community.

ELEVEN C'S FOR A STRONG MARRIAGE

CHAPTER 3

Communication

*Life is a series of communication links.
Questions unlock the links.*

Chapter 3

Communication

A Conversation about how to Talk Right

According to a secular Gallup poll report: "In an era of increasingly fragile marriages, a couple's ability to communicate is the single most important contributor to a stable and satisfying marriage."

Story: We both wrote our University of South African exams at the South African Consulate General in Chicago. This made for a few fun trips each year to the windy city. We would search online for a hotel and some exciting activities in the area and try to get a great deal. It always became a vacation adventure.

This particular time Rod was writing, and I was going to take Tamryn to a few hands-on exhibits. I thought Sheds Aquarium was a good idea. After all it was just a short taxi ride from where Rod was working his brain cells. I communicated with Rod the plan, and we covered the meeting spot and end time.

Later I found out that Rod had completed his exam and headed to the rendezvous place and found 'Nobody!' He told me he was not concerned as I would just call him. Cell phones and cell contracts were relatively new, and we both had just got new equipment and contracts. He tried to make contact. Nothing. He checked his phone. Nothing. Now unlike myself, Rod can be a bit of a worrier. But by now, we were more than 30 minutes past the meeting time, and I was still unable to make contact with him. For

Rod, the sun setting turned his mild worry and all the news articles about child and family abductions and the sex trade into a perceived reality.

What he did not know was I had secured a cab, pre Uber days, and had asked to be dropped off on Michigan Avenue. I was unfortunately unaware that there is a South Michigan Avenue and a North Michigan Avenue - 2 miles apart! I climbed out of the cab as the sun was setting and turned around and did not recognize a thing! My toddler had fallen asleep from the active day, so now I am lost, it's dark, I am carrying my kid and panic started setting in.

A jovial looking lady, sent by God, must have read my stressed and tearful face and helped me get re-orientated and head in the right direction. Now over an hour from our meeting time.

Rod was now redlining and telling himself that the worst had happened. He believed that his family was kidnapped. He began running around Chicago trying to track and trace our steps, looking for unmarked vehicles and guys with mean looking eyes, perhaps a big beard, because all villains have beards apparently. He went back to the Sheds Aquarium, but now it was closed. He ran to the parking garage to see if we went to the vehicle, then again to the Consulate General. By now 2 hours had passed. Night had set in and no communication.

Rod was now trying to phone anybody and was just working on missing persons contact and local 911 to desperately make contact. On the edge of a mental, physical and emotional breakdown, and three hours after our meeting time, I came

> **Communication is distorted by many things, so a translation is necessary, but that translating is fraught with challenges. Be aware that there is no clear and perfect communication.**

into view, tired, tearful and carrying my daughter walking down South Michigan Avenue.

It was only then that Rod discovered that he switched his phone off of roaming to save money and since we were in Chicago it rendered his phone utterly useless and I had been trying to make contact with him for hours! Needless to say after some tears and hugs, I shared with him a piece of my mind! Communication is key!

Life is a series of communication links. We are designed to relate. We are born in a community to interact with a community. That is one reason we are blessed with our five senses. We are supposed to communicate with one another and with God. The third conversation is about Communication.

> **Life is a series of communication links. We are designed to relate.**

We talk with ourselves

I noticed an interesting fact about communication; we are actually communicating with ourselves, all the time.

As you are reading this, you are making decisions and having arguments and conversations in your own mind. You are processing, intersecting, engaging and deciding on the truth of what you are reading. You are interacting with the material to bring it all into your context and world. That is a healthy, normal and expected activity. Your mind is continuously looking for data and processing it. So when it comes to communication, it is essential to be aware of how much contextual framing you are doing. How much internal dialogue you are assuming and most importantly how many perceptions you are drawing into the situation that may or may not be appropriate. You do not know the truth

COMMUNICATION

until you hear it and even when you hear it, you actually do not understand 100% of what is being spoken.

Action: Stop for a moment and listen to your head. I know this sounds strange, but become aware of the discussions you are having inside you so that you can notice it and be aware.

> You will never translate 100% of what is being said.

Our body talks too

I began to become more and more aware of how my gut feels when I am trying to make a decision. I ask God to guide me and, after some prayer, will attempt to see how I am reacting to the thoughts of my ponderings. If I have an uneasiness, I will try to temper my desire to move forward.

Action: Now pay attention to your gut, another source of information. Make a note of your feelings and thoughts. Are you joy-filled, relaxed, anxious, scared? What are you telling yourself right now, from your core or your gut? Maturity and wisdom help us discern between gut, (your feelings) and fear responses (adrenaline and anxiety).

We talk with our mouth

I sometimes have no clue what Cheryl is saying! I hear the words, I think I get it, and it's not till later I discover I was not even in the same country of understanding. Verbal communication goes like this. I have a thought, an idea. I then

> Communication is paramount for the effective growing, loving, learning and uniting of the couple.

try to find the best words, framing, illustrations, and argument to bring it to you. I am seated within my context, experience, back story, and worldview, so I present to you my correspondence from that launch pad. The message travels through the air and the differences between us. While it moves, much of the present environment is impacting your thinking. In other words, as it goes, there is some refraction and deviation caused by the very air it travels through. The air here is the relational space and thoughts of those communicating. Everything from the burrito you had for breakfast, to the irritating squeal of the Subway(Underground) running on the tracks. As you cling to the words being said, the ambient noises call for your attention. You vaguely hear 'mind the gap', over the loudspeakers, as you attempt to understand the message being communicated to you. Today these could be in any form, but for this illustration let's assume we are in the same train car together and you can hear me. My words, phrases, and language choice will come from my history. They will enter your head, and you will begin deciphering them and trying to discover what I mean, irrespective of what I said.

    You will translate and respond.

    Have you seen that Youtube video where a person is speaking in English to another nationality that speaks another dialect? You can see on the video that the person does not understand. You see the original communicator get up close and personal and now louder and more aggressively yells at the person exactly the same sentence. The apparent assumption is the louder you shout, the more easily people of other cultures and tongues can grasp what you are saying.

    I find it so amusing (or sad) that couples try this same technique. More

> **The louder you shout, does not enhance communicatio.**

about this in Chapter 4 on how to 'Fight Right.'

You will never translate 100% of what is being said. Yes, I said it twice! There is just too much interference, too much white noise, too many presuppositions, too much of a context chasm to bridge, never mind the gender gap. You will hear something of what is said and then assume, to fill in the gaps.

Perhaps you will ask some good questions to gain a fuller understanding. We have found that most people will ask about two or three probing questions to gain understanding, then give up. They become too embarrassed to ask again, so they will assume that they now know enough or develop their own construction of the situation in their mind. Most people will respond from their own perspective often without a comprehensive grasp of the original communiqué.

This can be devastating to a marriage. Communication is paramount for the active growing, loving, learning and uniting of a couple.

Here are some common hang-ups to good communicating. Obviously being a perfect couple we have never had any of these:

Learned communicating patterns

Learned patterns can be communication killers. We are very unaware of how much of our functioning and form is adopted from friends and family. Have you noticed how you sometimes begin to laugh like your boss or closest friend? Or use words that are common to your peer group? Talking about copy and paste, the

> **Learned or adopted communication patterns can be communication killers.**

more we age, the more we become like our parents. It astounds us every time. We are sorry that last statement should have come with a lifetime of free counseling sessions.

This is so prevalent. Experts believe between eighty and ninety percent of our life, we're actually operating on the unconscious level. Most of our interactions are unconscious. We emulate attributes from our parents, galvanized into us when we were young, through our lives.

Some of these learned patterns also result from our back story and manifest in our lives as 'beaten paths.' Tracks we slide into. Ways we respond and even emotions that we muster based on whether we feel threatened, insecure, afraid, vulnerable, fearful, confident, etc. These are auto controls that manifest before we even have a chance to adequately analyze them. The same thinking is what athletes call muscle memory. Your body reacts without consulting your brain. Think about how this works in the context of marriage. Fear just gripped your heart, did it not?

> Most of our interactions are unconscious. We inherit attributes from our parents when we're infants and toddlers. Your body reacts without consulting your brain.

Action: Take a moment to think about the way your parents communicated with each other. It is possible that the same things that frustrate you about their model may, in fact, be part of your own communication style?

You will be exercising love when, in your communication with your neighbor or spouse, you choose to understand their words from their perspective. Especially before you react out of pride, power or presupposition, i.e. from your perspective.

COMMUNICATION

Story: Speaking of understanding from her perspective. I was running hard in my demanding and busy weekday when Cheryl interrupted my rhythm to say her car had broken down.

I take care of the vehicles so, when I got the call that my wife had absolutely shredded a front right tire of the family van, I was instantly infuriated! I went from zero to red in three seconds. If one were a responsible driver, one would always do a 360 walk around to see if any tires need a touch of air and make sure the vehicle is mechanically sound. That tiny time inconvenience would now be saving me the significant tire expenses. Spending money on a repair verses replacing a whole set of front tires causes two different sets of reactions! My words were harsh, and accusations mean. I grumbled and growled as I negotiated the tow truck, tire replacements, and rescheduled our family transportation. After all, I work, and my responsibilities are demanding. I am vindicated in my fury.

It was not one week later, I was driving my vehicle, when I heard this strange sound. The car began to pull to the right. I immediately pulled over, and, to my shock and horror, the front right tire had blown! There were rubber and tire pieces everywhere along with my pride and ego. I had to place that call. Cheryl came to my rescue and just smiled without needing to say anything. Cheryl-1, Rodney-0.

> Learning from each other means the gloves are down.

Dean Sherman puts it like this,

"If I am humble and you are humble we will relate."

If I am in a condition that I am poised to learn from you, my gloves are down, and my heart is open. If not, my guns are ready, my sights are set in, my armor is on. I am charged before you even open your mouth!

Action: Ponder an example when you have allowed pride or power hunger to overtake your dialogue. When do you feel intimidated or weak in conversation? Some possible indicators or markers are anger or withdrawal. In these moments you might be guarding your heart, making you unable to be open-handed and open-hearted. Protecting your heart should be left to God.

A goal of marriage: overcome selfishness

To move from selfishness to become selfless is one of the ultimate reasons for marriage, but also its greatest struggle. Let us dip into some more theology: The fall of mankind, the day that sin became part of who we are, began with a selfish seed. Selfishness pumped through the veins of Adam and Eve as they disobeyed God and responded to satan. This is a narrative captured for us in Genesis 3. A quick read will show how selfishness prevailed over selflessness.

We will all continue to fight this magnetic pull all our lives.

The flesh in us, our humanness, pulls continuously towards self while the Holy Spirit of God pulls towards selfless sacrifice. (To become like Jesus Christ, refer

> In marriage you can migrate into selfish behavior or you can nurture self-sacrifice. Welcome to the continuous cycles of marriage maturity.

to the first chapter). Marriage is the perfect incubator for either of these attitudes to flourish. Here you can migrate into selfish behavior or you can nurture self-sacrifice. Have you ever felt like a hero one moment and within the hour a jerk? Welcome to the continuous cycles of marriage maturity that has its conclusion only when you stand before God.

Neglecting God's perspective

I often forget that Jesus died for Cheryl and, I think she forgets, He did the same for me. That is the same for the person you are communicating with. He or she is so valuable that Jesus give His life for them. Have you pondered that? If they were only worth a cow, then God would have only had to sacrifice a cow! If they are worth His death, should we not treat them and every other human differently. If our spouse is a gift to God, should we really be breaking them down and destroying them, no matter how poorly they are communicating and no matter what kind of buttons they are pushing? You can win the battle and lose the war. This reminds me of a line in the musical *'Annie Get Your Gun'* by Dorothy Fields and Herbert Fields, where the lead female actress has to lose the battle to win the man.

> **Remember the person has God value.**

Action: How does this make you feel if you reflect on the last argument you had with your spouse to be? What would you think if we were able to capture that scene 'reality show' style, and put it on Youtube? How do you want this to look in the future?

Remember how important communication was/is while you were/are dating?

Rod's Story: I remember writing long romantic snail mail letters. Running up huge phone bills, before unlimited calling. I must also confess, cheating the public 'call box' with a hanging coin to speak for hours on the local telephone company dime. When we were dating, I used to sneak out of the house, late at night. This SWOT exercise included disconnecting the actual windows and unscrewing the security and burglar bars. I would then walk, run or ride my bicycle 4 miles to knock on her window and stand having conversations for hours about, well, nothing. Then traveling all the way back to crawl back into the house and then to sleep for a couple of hours before heading to school or work. Talking, hanging out, communicating, and just being with each other was so fulfilling. Until we got married.

Attention Span

We have become superficial. Moving from deep thinkers, people with time to ponder, absorb, and reflect. We have forgotten the value of silence, long walks, sunsets, and building plastic model planes. We have become over-stimulated, over-busy, over-resourced, profoundly disconnected, multi-tasked, rushed, harassed individuals. The very length of a discussion, the concentration of a dialogue (to understand), seems way too much for us.

Even a cursory greeting is shortened and often not replied to. Hello is now 'hey', Ok is now 'k'. Having a long dinner with a meaningful conversation, with someone we love, almost seems impossible without

> **We are superficial. We have moved from deep thinkers to become over stimulated, highly disconnected, individuals.**

checking our social media status and posting at least one picture. The world, and most of the 1,247 active 'friends' you have, simply must know you are eating a burger by romantic candlelight at your local spot. I'm sure they stopped what they were doing to marvel.

Communication content

Talking is part of communicating. It encompasses at the very least words, sounds, inflections, and nonverbal signals. The use of words, the structure of the sentences and their delivery play a vital role in accurate understanding. The very sound of your voice can turn a question into a statement. One needs to become acutely aware of how powerful words are. Proverbs 12:18 puts it like this

> *"The words of the reckless pierce like swords, but the tongue of the wise brings healing."*

Words can build up and words can tear down. It is effortless to use words as weapons and be totally unaware of the effect they have on others. For some people, words can carry them for days or weeks or even months depending on what is said.

> **Words can build up and words can break down. It is very easy to use words as weapons and be totally unaware of the effect on others.**

Rod's Story: I was recently at a funeral where a handwritten letter was read. It was written by the deceased before his cancer ate away at his body. This note from a loving dad and husband was written for his wife and family. The words were warm, the lines well crafted, the message personal, the tears real, and the heart exposed. Each word was a word of love, affirmation, encouragement, and motivation. He spoke directly and intimately, he mentioned personal names and listed personal situations. Those words will last a lifetime. He crafted the words carefully over his decline. Final words are remembered forever and impact those left behind.

The way words are presented can do a tremendous amount for a discussion. The tone and sound of our voices can tell a story before the first sentence is complete. Often breathing in and out a few times will calm a heart rate and open an attitude to being flexible in the upcoming dialogue.

Then there are *nonverbal cues*. We say more with our bodies and our mannerisms than with our choice of words or our tone of voice. In fact, experts believe up to 70% of meaning in communication is conveyed nonverbally. Leaning in says 'interest', arms folded can indicate disinterest, a cocked head can indicate attitude or confusion, rolling eyes disdain, etc. Gesticulations can bring home a point but can also be seen as aggressive or demanding. Remember, the person hears more than you say. A smile can change the entire dialogue. We find that we are more apt to be receptive and engaged when we are relaxed and jovial, after all, most motivational speakers will begin with a joke or a funny illustration. Sometimes our brains have to tell our faces to project a good message.

> **We hear more than is said.**

Listening

Active listening is a skill one has to spend a lifetime developing. The average dialogue between a husband and a wife will be filled with defensive poise and childish behaviors. The mature person will strive

> **Active listening is a skill that one has to spend a lifetime developing.**

to really hear the person that is laying their heart out on the line. Taking the action step of 'repeating back' what you have listened to is very helpful when navigating a touchy subject or just seeking clarity.

Cheryl's Story: I remember the time Rod was asked to speak at a senior center. Listening in the audience was a retired senior pastor. Within a few seconds, he was snoring.

Not surprisingly he ran a little late in his preparation so, in his youthful zeal and inexperience, he decided to rework and use an old youth group sermon on promiscuity and lust. At the end of the active presentation, with gesticulations, illustrations, cross-references and scriptural unpacking, the former pastor awoke. He pushed his wheelchair to the exit and thanked Rod for an impacting, inspiring and life-changing message. Overhearing the accolades our dear family could not contain themselves, and quickly exited the building exploding in laughter. You know the kind that makes you snort and slobber. There were conversations and thoughts of running through the halls and warning all the unsuspecting geriatric grannies that lust was on the loose! Rod vetoed it!

A few bad listening habits to avoid

Interrupter: One of the worst is demonstrated by the interrupter. Before Cheryl can structure the sentence, I will begin my rebuttal. The interrupter jumps in without even trying, for a moment, to understand or allow the person to finish their thought. Interrupters assume they know what the other person is about to say and send the dangerous message: "what you say has little

> **Avoid typical bad listening habits.**

value to me." Interrupters then think what to say, before trying to understand what is being said. They cannot possibly grasp your full perspective while focused on their defenses.

Completer: These people like to finish what you are saying, of which I am the worst. After all I know what Cheryl should want to say, right? No matter how predictable your comments may be, completing sentences shows great disrespect for the speaker and a great arrogance by the 'listener'. This sends the dangerous message: "you are not smart enough to know what you are saying. I know better."

Rambler: Here is the long-winded person who tests the patience of the listener. An excellent approach to ramblers (some like the scenic route) is merely to inform them that covering so much with so many words tends to lose you. Cover one topic at a time and allow feedback every few sentences. This will really help communication. This sends the dangerous message: "only my words have value, you are only here to enjoy my brilliance"

Topic changer: I (Cheryl) am a master at this. There are just so many things on my mind, and everything is connected. I struggle to stay on one topic at a time. I really am one who begins a conversation talking about the cost of firewood and ends on world peace. Know where you are going with the discussion. When dealing with this, Rod will try to ask me to be clear and address each topic at a time. The secret here is to remember the other 'tabled' issues and to make sure that we discuss them at a later stage. Make sure they are not forgotten.

The environment

The environment plays a role in this listening process. Meeting in a mall might be nice for a romantic cup of coffee and some idle chit-chat. When dealing with deep, personal and invasive discussions a more intimate private place may be necessary. Intentional, clear time (I have to rush in 5) with no distractions, will enhance the communicative process and will empower the listener for crisp understanding. Clear eye contact, clear space (no screaming kids, TV, etc.)

> Clear eye contact, clear space, clear time, will enhance the communication process and will empower the listener for crisp understanding.

Good communication demands time:
Quality and quantity time. Spending lots of time with the one that you love should be a pleasure. Resulting in opportunity to cover fun topics and laughter. If every time you 'chat' you are dealing with an issue, the color soon drains out of the relationship. Delight more, be silly more, do fun things, more. Risk a little and talk about it with much frivolity and expression. You need the quality time to move through growth issues, but you need the quantity to deepen and enrich the relationship.

Make a note of the best times during the day, week and month to communicate. After a long work day, a spouse might be tired and drained from many exhausting dialogues. It might take time for him or her

> You need the quality time to move through growth issues but you need the quantity to deepen and enrich the relationship.

to detox from their busy day before they can be fully present for your discussion. Attacking someone at the door as they enter seldom will lead to cooperative communication. Regular communication throughout the day will allow deliberately allocated time to become moments of deeper interaction and conversation.

> Good communication needs time.

One can also improve one's communication skills by knowing about the natural mood and pressure swings of your spouse. Things like lack of sleep, midlife crisis, menstrual cycle, menopause, sexual frustrations are a few examples of times when communication will be different.

Rod's Story: Pornography is right for your marital intimacy he said, watch it together he said, you will spice things up, he said. These were the words of my ministry reverend and authority when we moved from our home town to a church in Middleberg, Mapumalanga, South Africa.

Dancing to the rhythms of the African Umfundisi (Ministers) during the local outreach, singing and playing in the newly remodeled church sanctuary, spelunking with the youth group, and planning and executing global mission trips were intoxicating. Time evaporated at the power of my addictions of acceptance and significance, and I paid for it in my marriage. It became starved of quality and quantity time. The first years of ministry were surrounded by friends, family, and home town mentors that quickly held us accountable to keep our priorities balanced. Immaturity cost us ties with some of the most reliant relationships and counsel. Time with Cheryl and our young firstborn was sparse at best. Add to that three days of training in the township of Soweto, South Africa, and we were charged for a pastoral collapse. I was oblivious, but Cheryl was hurting!

By the grace of God, we received a call to the United States that saved us from a horrid and legacy altering calamity. God stopped us! We were now more than ever dependent on each other. 'I remember sitting in a McDonald's after we just arrived,' Cheryl said, 'and I did not even know what to say to you. We had not spoken or had one-on-one time for so long.' We had become strangers. Thankfully we were exposed to great mentoring in Pastor Jim Govatos and others, great teachings like the Five Love Languages by Dr. Chapman[1] and Laugh Your Way to a Better Marriage by Mark Gungor[2]. We now spend time together in the discovery of each other and our unique ways to love one another. It took quality and quantity time.

Questions are the golden keys to understanding

Develop the habit of always beginning with a question. This will help reframe your reference to one of 'seeking to understand' and not to interrupt, defend, attack or simply be understood. Often when you have been together for some time, you might just assume you already know. You might arrogantly believe you can both finish their statement and answer it for them. Why not try to hear and understand the deeper feelings that are going on behind the conversation, or outburst. Peeling back the onion. Often the first things said are not meant, or are not even the reason for the discussion. Some examples of questions that develop understanding:

> **Questions are the golden keys to understanding.**

- Is this hard for you? Why?
- What is causing a 10 response when this looks like it could be a 2 or 3, help me understand what is making this so painful for you?

- Your anger seems unrelated to the issue, please help me understand how you see the situation?
- I can see that you are hurt, please help me understand how I have hurt you?

Action: Get your kneecaps together and enter carefully into 'touchy' communication. Talk about something that has been 'off limits' but lean into it with the attempt to hear the other person's perspective. Make it carry more value than your own. Climb into their moccasins (shoes). Make some notes of how this went. Were you able to listen without interrupting? Were you able to mine the dialogue for the real issues or underlying reasons? Were you able to ask questions to foster understanding? Were you able to see the situation through their eyes? Remember this is not a fight. That is the next chapter.

God is a great communicator

God communicates today! He spoke in Genesis, and the world was created. John 1 reminds us:

> *"In the beginning was the Word, and the Word was with God, and the Word was God. He was with God in the beginning."*

God placed His presence amongst the people in different ways throughout the Old Testament. One was the place of the Holy of Holies in the temple, another was on Mount Sinai with Moses, etc. Later, God communicated through sending His Son Jesus, who walked and talked and spoke to

> God communicates today! This gives us the advantage of tapping into divine wisdom in conversation.

humanity directly.

Imagine you are walking along the beachfront and you come across a number of small rock pools. These crystal clear aquariums are full of fish and sea life trapped because of the receding tide. When you place your hand in the water, do you notice how the fish scatter with fear? But other fish and sea creatures move freely in and out of the ecosystem unperturbed because they have on them the same or similar 'skin'. These new visitors become an attraction as the locals peep from under shells and plants and approach with inquisitive interest.

This was God's plan in sending Jesus. God could have come himself and invaded the world and we would have all scattered in fear. However, just like the fish in the tidal pools, they are drawn towards the new visitor, in much the same way God took on flesh, in the form of Jesus Christ. His desire was for the same result, so we would not fear but be inquisitive and explore. We find this described in John 1 verse 14

'The Word became flesh and made his dwelling among us. We have seen his glory, the glory of the one and only Son, who came from the Father, full of grace and truth.'

He called a group of men around Himself and became deeply connected to them and their lives. He interacted and taught the locals, sharing the Divine plan of redemption for a fallen world. He invested Himself highly in those He came into contact with by meeting needs and pointing to the Father God.

After Jesus was raised from the dead, He then sent His Holy Spirit so all humankind could be in regular communication with God, not just those who knew Jesus in his physical form. Communication is critical for God. This gives us the advantage of tapping into divine wisdom in conversation. Asking the Holy Spirit to guide your words and actions will enlist the power and presence of the Creator of the universe into your interaction. Imagine the resources you can now call on to help you understand others, especially your spouse. You are calling on God in person!

Some thoughts on some bad communication

Avoid negative self-talk: that seems to dominate our personal verbal landscape. We seem to run ourselves down daily. Look in the mirror and get as motivated about you as God is! Matthew 12 verse 36:

> "But I tell you that everyone will have to give account on the day of judgment for every empty word they have spoken."

> Avoid bad communication: Negative self-talk, crass and degrading words and empty words.

Avoid crass and degrading words: swearing at your spouse achieves little. It might indicate your lack of vocabulary or your lack of self-control, but it naturally will not enhance your goal to understand or be understood. Repeating the same words you learned from your sailor friends, hardly seems productive. The Bible guides us in Colossians 3 verse 8 to 10:

> "But now you must also rid yourselves of all such things as these: anger, rage, malice, slander, and filthy language from your lips. Do not lie to each other, since you have taken off your old self with its practices and have put on the new self, which is being renewed in knowledge in the image of its Creator."

COMMUNICATION

Avoid empty words: I think of those as comments under your breath that achieve nothing besides "scoring" exit points against a verbal sparring partner. Those hand grenades can cause more damage than the sense of satisfaction they seem to bring in the moment. Take note of Ephesians 4 verse 29:

> *"Do not let any unwholesome talk come out of your mouths, but only what is helpful for building others up according to their needs, that it may benefit those who listen."*

Talk well, talk a lot, talk to each other. This is a person that wants to marry you because they actually like being around you. The beauty of this grows through time.

> **Let's learn how to talk to each other.**

ELEVEN C'S FOR A STRONG MARRIAGE

Speed Notes on Chapter 3

- A couple's ability to communicate is the single most important contributor to a stable and satisfying marriage.
- We talk with ourselves, we talk with our mouths and our bodies 'talk' too.
- If I am humble and you are humble we will relate.
- Marriage moves a person from selfishness to self*less*ness, this is its greatest struggle and the greatest victory, and this happens in cycles over a *lifetime*.
- Remember the person you are communicating with, Jesus died on the cross for them, *that is their value*, so how should we treat them?
- Keep it simple, keep it clear, and note we have almost lost our ability to think deeply.
- Words are powerful, be wise *as* you use them, be wise *how* you use them and be wise *if* you use them.
- Active listening is an art form that one must *learn* to master.
- The context and environment will impact the result. You need time and space for each other, a quick texted message is not deep communicating, but is helpful if you late for dinner.
- God is the best communicator, ask him to help you as you move into deep, meaningful and compelling communication. (Luke 12:12 "or the Holy Spirit will teach you at that time what you should say.")

Action Steps

- Have a date and begin a happy conversation making a note of everything you have learned. Make it something simple, like 'How was your day?", or 'What would you like to do for the weekend?', or 'What is something you have always dreamed of doing, but not been able?' Take note of how easy it is to move 'into your own head.' Observe how you 'listen waiting to speak' instead of trying to hear and understand. This is not the time to correct or respond to him or her, but to reflect on your own style, emotions, behavior, reactions, and responses. Be nice!
- Together read the book the Five Love Languages by Dr. Gary Chapman[1] and complete the quiz to discover each other.
- Write out your spouse's Love Language on a piece of paper and place it in your Bible, refer to it daily and ponder a way to make him/her feel loved.
- Exercise the spiritual discipline of *Prayer.*

ELEVEN C'S FOR A STRONG MARRIAGE

CHAPTER 4

Conflict

*Couples should fight!
Conflict is God's way of illuminating
yourself to yourself!*

Chapter 4

Conflict

A Conversation about how to Fight Right!

Husbands and wives fight, *and we should!* Let us talk about the fourth conversation, **Conflict**.

> **Couples should fight, conflict is part of daily life.**

Story: Cheryl and I fight. I remember one particular trip we made to the ski slopes on the Stubai Glacier in Austria. Let us set the context. Cheryl hates heights. We had to take a bus, then a train, then a cable car just to get there. We began at the crack of dawn, and it took most of the morning. As the day was progressing, my excitement was building, (think 3 year old in a candy store excited,) and hers was waning.

The loft and angles of the transportation increased the closer we got to the lodge. The romantic notion of a Royal family style picture dissipated. The image of the fluffy white fresh packed powder snow slopes contrasted against the bright colors of our ski gear. It was developing into my picture perfect day but in reality melting into Cheryls worst nightmare. Maybe tossing a lump of cold snow down her jacket did not help much.

Gear on, clipped in, we headed for the lifts. I suggested we go right to the top, after all, how hard could it be? Cheryl wanted to begin on the smaller bunny hills with all the 4 and 5-year-olds. After a rather robust conversation, I convinced her and we headed up, although she did not seem motivated.

CONFLICT

With some difficulty we boarded the ski lift. I remember something about the operator having to shut the whole thing down while I scrambled to gain my footing, get my body on the seat and grabbed and dragged Cheryl onto the ride before she could change her mind.

And we were off. Raising higher and higher above the groomed surfaces as we headed to the top. The cold was now outside and sitting next to me! What does a double black diamond ski slop mean anyway?

We unceremoniously plopped off at the top and surveyed the dramatic drop of the glacial mountain. It looks far higher, steeper, and scarier from this vantage point. But hey, it's easy right? Just zig-zag left and right. You can go whatever speed you want. At this point, Cheryl was done. All her energy was gone. I, being the loving husband I am, encouraged her with some 'professional' instruction and a little nudge.

There were a few dynamics I had not considered. Firstly when one is new at this sport, trying to get the long skies to behave is a challenge. So when my lovely wife turned to go downhill, the zig and zag was just not happening. She only gained speed and momentum. At this point, she was flying, screaming and flapping. Secondly, how was I to know the taped off sections were dangerous crevasse and not short cuts? Let me further define. It is a place where the glacier ice surface has separated, and a fissure has opened up. Some of these can be 350 feet deep. Thirdly, I could not anticipate Cheryl would not follow my unequivocally clear instructions to sit down if she had any crises.

The result; she flew down the slope and fell. He knee twisted as her legs went in one direction and her body another. The tissue instantly began swelling. She eventually stopped about 10 feet from the clearly marked caution tapped deep hole that would have undoubtedly killed her.

Now tearful, in pain, and having just seen her life flash before her eyes, she was not in the mood to hear analysis and critique of her winter sports style. She was fuming! She grabbed her gear and stomped all the way down to the lodge where she remained for the rest of the afternoon. I just had to keep going because it was already paid for and I did not want to waste. Needless to say, I got an earful, and even a hot chocolate could not temper.

I think those couples that 'never fight' potentially have one of two situations playing out:

- One of the partners is a doormat or does not have the self-confidence to have an opinion. They become trampled on, or neutered, by the other. They are not allowed to have another or contrasting perspective.

- There is no passion between the couple because if they ever disagree they will destroy utopia in the relationship. This is an unsaid statement.

The truth is, conflict arises when expectations do not match the harsh reality and pain of the world. Throw in personality, childhood templates, and all the unique aspects of the human experience and you will discover conflict as a regular part of living. Sometimes caused by the most simple, or alternatively by deeply layered and involved striations from the past.

We have noticed often, in our marriage, conflict can be attributed to an old wound or perception. Sometimes it actually

> **We assume that we know what others are thinking. We fill in the blanks with our very own perceived reality.**

CONFLICT

has nothing to do with our present issue but a build-up of pressure, fear, anxiety from other sources. Most often it can be attributed to fear. An example could be work, parents, etc.

We live in a profoundly self-indulged and entitled world, so the atmosphere is super-charged against humble hearing and understanding of others anyway. We are all swimming upstream, from the minute we meet. The wrestle between our own understanding of ourselves, and our attempt to move beyond that, to understand another human being. This is at times an almost impossible venture.

Dynamics like a wide age-spread, a multi-cultural partnership, a second marriage, kids and different temperaments heightens the struggle. Add to that contrasting love languages (gifts, words, time, service or touch: taken from the Five Love Languages by Dr. Gary Chapman), make conflict an inevitability in every relationship.

Cheryl's Story: Rod ran really hard trying to prove himself as the new youth pastor, as we had just arrived in the States. This left me and our first born, Tamryn, often alone at home. We hosted a small group on a Friday afternoons in our home. He would come flying home to run the vacuum cleaner over the house to get everything ready for the guests. Rod had grown up in a home where love was tied together with service. 'If you love me you will mow the lawn.'

I would get irritated. He was not sitting with me having a cup of coffee and investing time in me. Due to the lack of intentional time with me, I would refuse to acknowledge his 'gallant' love gestures of service. He wanted me to shower him with kind words, his love language. Conflict was predictable,

> **Conflict is God's way of illuminating yourself to yourself.**

69

just before Bible study!

Dr. Chapman's book opened our eyes to this 'perfect storm' scenario. This was life-changing!

Conflict is, a gift from God. You will fight all your married life, but that is intentional. It is God's way of illuminating yourself to yourself. It is in conflict situations that your mask is off and the real you is presenting, without the opportunity to cover up or be politically correct. This does not sound very desirable, but conflict can be the most enlightening and liberating part of marriage. If you were broken, would you not want to know? Let's bring this concept home. If your zipper was down would you not want to be informed, before the end of the day?

There is hope. The Bible is clear in Philippians 4 verse 13:

"we can do all things through Christ who strengthens us."

But there is a part we play in this equation. We have to desire to resolve the conflict. But here it is. *We always bring ourselves to the conflict we are in.*

> **We always bring ourselves to the very conflict that we are in.**

Assuming that the other person is wrong and with enough shouting, manipulating, explaining and justifying they will eventually see it your way. This is the worst way to enter a dialogue. We move straight down the road of trouble when we assume that we understand the other person. We sometimes even imagine what they are thinking, meaning and wanting. We fill in the blanks with our perceived reality. We seldom take the time to understand what has caused the other person's stresses. We might not even listen to them because we are too ready to correct and enlighten them.

We will migrate into self-defense quickly when feeling incapable of resolving the issue or exposed as inadequate to handle the situation. As a man, I am astounded how easily I can feel emasculated and threatened. That is like adding fuel to the flames.

Story: One of our first dates was 'dinner and a movie.' I have to admit, I was running a touch late. It became 'movie and a dessert.' The movie was romantic and the atmosphere perfect. After the final curtain, we headed down to the local sweet treat hangout, called "The Spur." We both ordered the infamous Banana Boat ice-cream and fruit salad parfait. Its size was only trumped by its reputation!

Looking lovingly into her eyes I scooped up a huge mouthful and shoveled it into my mouth. Instead of a beautiful, bursting bouquet of flavor, I discovered rancid fruit. Due to the warm African climate and non existent restaurant etiquette, the fresh fruit had been allowed to turn during the day and was now rotten.

Now, being one of our first dates, I was too embarrassed to enter into the conversation to check if her order was the same. I came up with a 'wonderful' plan. Polish mine off and get a taste of hers. I know, a rotten plan ... literally! At the time, for some reason, it seemed to make perfect sense.

Choking down my fruit and ice-cream, I began eating on her desert only to discover the same vile taste. To this day we laugh at our lack of communication and ability to handle conflict. We ended the night bloated on bad fruit, bubbling over with love, but unable to lean into a real conversation.

We believe that conflict is necessary, expected, and

even beneficial. Each and every moment of passionate and robust interaction is a moment to learn about yourself and your spouse. A discerning listener will find many nuggets of wisdom in all the human dialogues and interactions faced every day. This reminds me of James 1 verse 2 to 4:

> "Consider it pure joy, my brothers and sisters, whenever you face trials of many kinds, because you know that the testing of your faith produces perseverance. Let perseverance finish its work so that you may be mature and complete, not lacking anything."

> **Each and every moment of strong and passionate interaction is a moment to learn about yourself and your spouse.**

There are ways to enter into conflict that will enhance the possibilities of learning, growing and maturing. Entering a conflict the wrong way only leads to a degrading, mud-slinging match. The results are predictably pain and bloodshed.

'Knowing how to fight fair is critical to survival of the marriage as happy couple' (Parrott 2006:119)[1]

Here are some tools we try to employ to 'Fight Right', even though we often fail:

First
Attack the problem not the person

Fight in a united way against the problem not each other. So for example, he is late from work and did not communicate with her. He feels tired and justified from a hard day. She feels ignored and devalued. The problem here could be the communication or lack thereof, and not the fact that he is late or she is disillusioned. Fight in a way to figure out how to communicate better with each other.

> **Fight in a united way against the problem not each other.**

Cheryl's Story: As a trained paramedic, Rod is never one to drive past any kind of emergency.

We were newly married, by just one day, and were traveling to our three-day honeymoon venue. This was back in the early nineties, pre-cellphone era. We were excited about this vacation, after the crazy run up to our wedding. We were chit-chatting, while we booked into our beachfront resort, as we received our room keys, we overheard that there had been a partial head-on collision with a minivan and farm truck just down the road. They were asking the front desk to call an ambulance and find help. 'Let's go,' was all I heard as Rod headed back out to the still packed car.

He did basic triage and proceeded to care for the broken and bleeding as best he could. I presumed we would be there for a few minutes, but no, 3 hours later!! It was now dark, cold, and the fun chit chat had cooled into selfish irritation. Help had arrived, but he *had to* wait until everything was 100 % before returning back to our luxury getaway.

Back at the venue, we were consumed with its beauty, and I began to relax. My anger at the rough start began to dissipate. Going through the pack of coupons and vouchers we were handed at registration, I was all over the good deals, and Rod was all over squeezing as much as he could out of each day. No sleeping in for us!

Day one: Free horseback riding! I had repeatedly told him I had never ridden and didn't think it was a good idea, but he insisted. My hands ended up blistered from my fear-filled sweaty grip on the reigns. My legs rubbed raw from squeezing the saddle so hard. This experience was not good for honeymooners, is all I'm going to say!

Day two: Free golf! Challenge one, we had never played before. Challenge two, gale force winds. But hey, it was free! My blistered hands were rebelling. You would think Rod would stop after 9, but no, 18 holes were included in the honeymoon deal! The whoosh and crack of our 'fun' early morning tee off concluded as the sun was setting. Rod did successfully lose a ball every hole. Finally on the last one he convinced me to give him my ball, the last one left, and the one I began with. Yep, you guessed it, with his now perfected slice, he lost that one too!

Day three: Our final day, I refused to do anything! I setup poolside with no intention of moving until our departure. I was sore, bruised, and not happy, wondering what was I thinking to say 'I do.' I had no idea even how to enter this 'fight.'

Second
Do not leave it

Do not get tricked into thinking because she is not yelling at you or he is not raising his voice that all is okay. Problems do not just disappear with time. They fester, they grow, and they rot, just like bad fruit. These avoidance patterns will only return to bring hurt and destruction later. We tend to pack them in our 'backpack' of thoughts and feelings to be used as ammunition at a future conflict. Over time they grow into consuming monsters. Our luggage we drag behind us can become quite full and daunt-

> Do not leave issues unattended, because avoidance will only result in more aggressive conflict later. This is a weak response.

ing. The Bible puts it this way in Ephesians 4 verse 26:

> *"In your anger do not sin: Do not let the sun go down while you are still angry."*

In other words, deal with it promptly. I would suggest within 24 hours, if possible. Bad news does not get better with time.

Third
Be aware of context

Enter into the conflict taking your spouse into consideration. Heading into a broad or demanding topic when they are clearly tired, busy, hungry, in pain or under extreme pressure is thoughtless and unloving. This will only place them in a defensive or aggressive poise. A better plan we found is to mention that you have an item that you want to address and plan a time to talk it through. Something like, *'Honey, I would like to talk to you about communication between us. When I got home late the other night and food was spoiled, it looked like you felt hurt. I do not want to do that to you. Can we talk about this after the kids go to sleep tonight?'*

> **Be aware of context, enter into conversation taking them into consideration.**

Some couples have to be very creative here. Their work schedules and home responsibilities can become so demanding that finding the time when s/he is not exhausted, hungry or depleted can be tough. Sometimes just getting in the same room can be a challenge. These couples might have to make some tough decisions or some significant investments, like a babysitter, to create the space and time to discover each other. If not the relationship will be based on

TV, eating and sleeping. Basically roommates with benefits.

According to an article published by Dr. Luisa Dillner, in the UK based, Guardian, *The Office for National Statistics* states on average we spend only two to two and half hours a day together, including weekends. We spend one-third of that time watching TV, 30 minutes eating, and 24 minutes doing housework together. Married people only spend half an hour more together than people who cohabit[2].

We try to be purposeful about the interaction. It takes focused intentionality about not only the approach but also the conversation. We should not try to discuss the budget through the toilet door, or solve the family schedule, three rooms over. Both of which we have done.

This all sounds well and good but what if things spiral out of control? What if a match is lit in the gas-filled room? Mark Gungor in his conference *'Laugh your way to a Better Marriage,'* says hit the Reset button. This is the moment when you stop! Where you become aware that more harm than good is coming from the conversation and pause. It is important to note this is merely a pause to, calm down and gain perspective. It is not for sweeping the conflict under the rug. Real men and loving women will be purposeful about re-engaging in the necessary follow-up conversation.

Fourth
Never generalize

Words like 'always,' 'all the time' and 'never,' are all the time, always, never helpful and quite frankly incorrect.

Fifth
Take note of patterns

> People use conversation patterns and techniques to create safe space or barriers of protection between themselves and the 'attacker'.

There might be a pattern of behavior that needs to be addressed, in a loving way. There are also patterns of fighting that need to be brought to the awareness of each other. Some typically destructive conflict modes include avoiding, attacking, demanding, criticizing, crying, accusing, withdrawing and the silent treatment. These are simply protection techniques. They are building a safe space or barrier between themselves and the 'attacker.' A wise spouse will notice the natural cause and effect and will be proactive about exposing this to their spouse.

Sixth
Deal with one thing at a time

Approaching someone you love, with a gun full of ammunition, will never achieve the desired result. A growing number of adults suffer from ADD and ADHD, and the thought of shooting buckshot at them will only ignite more war. Focus on just one topic at a time, and yes, other thoughts will come into your mind during this conflict. Just write them down or make a mental note and come back to them another time. One topic at a time has a far greater opportunity for resolve. Attacking someone by bringing up multiple issues all at once will more likely to result in a defensive poise and casualties.

Seventh
Use 'I' language not 'You' language

When you are telling the other person 'You did this', and 'you did that,' immediately you are being accusatory. A better approach is to say 'I feel this when you did that' or 'help me understand why you did this or that, so I might better understand you.' This *'help me understand'* statement has enlightened me to a lot of things I would have otherwise missed had I just resorted to responding.

> 'Help me understand' statement has enlightened me to a lot of things that I would have missed had I just resorted to rage.

Eighth
One will always win the words war

One spouse will always be quicker with their tongue than the other. The one who is sharp-tongued needs to be aware of this. Psalm 63 verse 4

> *'They sharpen their tongues like swords and aim cruel words like deadly arrows.'*

This is when that reset button is so important. It is imperative, when things get out of hand, for both parties to respect and call for a 'reset.' This is done out of love. Resorting to guerrilla warfare, by dropping a grenade and running, produces only casualties and pain. You could win the battle, but loose the war.

> Words can build up and break down. It is easy to use words as weapons and be totally unaware of the effect.

Ninth
Have eye contact

Talking to someone three rooms and two doors away, while they are consumed with another task, might seem like efficient multitasking. It is not! When one talks to a child, you will likely ask them to look at you. This is how you know you have their attention. The kid wants to look down, a wise father will say, "Look here son," so that the boy can see into the father's eyes that the words he is about to tell are accurate and trustworthy. In the same way, eye contact in a marriage conflict indicates importance, love, openness, transparency, truthfulness, intimacy, priority and more. How do you feel when you are talking to someone, who is consumed with their laptop?

Tenth
Call for a 'Conflict Conversation'

One: Ask yourself the question, is this a 'me' thing or is this a 'them' thing? Is this something that comes out of your own story, the wounds of your own past? Are these unmet expectations or frustrations? Have you transported you work stresses home? Did the nightly new get to you? Your reaction may have nothing to do with your loved one, it might really just be something you are processing from your day. This is important to decipher.

> **Is this a ME thing, or is this a THEM thing?**

Story: We wanted high-speed internet. Our house was situated in the country and would need an aerial tower to receive the strongest signal. I consulted my technically advanced and digitally savvy friend Aaron, who was already 'online.' His signal was good, but his tower was about 10 feet short for a great signal, he confirmed our need and so began the great tower adventure.

Aaron had a buddy who happened to have one lying in his back yard. We headed over to see if it might work and saw what appeared to be a perfect fit. Interestingly enough it was going to be about 10 feet higher than Aaron's tower. I thought about it. I wanted those extra 10 feet. The higher the tower the less interruption and the better signal for me, right?

After some dangerous assembly attempts, we got our neighbor, Steve, to help us erect the monstrosity. I was happy, pompous and proud of my mega achievement. Step back ACJB World Radio, we're going live!

I thought again about my friend and his tower height issues. I quickly ignored that silly thought. I wanted all the reach I could get. I wanted a more prominent tower because bigger is better.

A few days passed and the internet company did the install while I was at work. They said they found the perfect spot on the tower for the best signal in the area. They assured us that we were going to be rocking high speed and streaming videos like there was no tomorrow. When I got home and took a look at the tower I noticed they placed the receiver exactly 10 feet down from the top. The top 10 feet of the pole was totally unused and, quite frankly, a neighborhood eye sore. I realized, had I been in a different place, if I had thought about his needs before mine, we could have found a win, win. I had a confession to make, which I did. We are friends to this day and still chuckle at my stupidity from time to time.

Two: Am I in the right place to enter into the conversation? Am I too tired, too irrational, too angry, too busy, etc? Am I more concerned with winning than listening? Am I more about getting my own way than understanding their way?

> You will want to be purposeful and strategic about the interaction.

Three: Does my spouse have space, right now, for this conversation? The kids were screaming, the food boiled over, they just drove over the cat, the grocery bag broke and spilled milk on Nana's old carpet, leaning in with "Hey honey, is this a good time to talk about our sex life?", might not get the desired results.

Four: Ask when is a suitable date and time. Typically 2-24 hours is a reasonable expectation. Purposeful planning means you want to engage in the conversation with Ephesians 4 verse 29-32 on your heart.

"Do not let any unwholesome talk come out of your mouths, but only what is helpful for building others up according to their needs, that it may benefit those who listen. And do not grieve the Holy Spirit of God, with whom you were sealed for the day of redemption. Get rid of all bitterness, rage and anger, brawling and slander, along with every form of malice. Be kind and compassionate to one another, forgiving each other, just as in Christ God forgave you."

Five: Hit the RESET BUTTON, if the conversation

is going south, agree upon a date and time to discuss the issue further. Treat this like you would a romantic date. It will be hard, but it will till the soil for an open dialogue.

> Her silence does not mean it's okay, lean in.

Six: Ask good questions. Good questions bring understanding. The other person experiences your care and love. The conversation becomes more about understanding them than proving your point.

Seven: Without being condescending, sarcastic or derogatory, reflect back what you are hearing. Repeating back the other person's words feels strange and unfamiliar at first but the more you do it, the better you become. This way you will begin to understand each other and really hear. Remember there is translating that is happening between what they say and what you hear, add to that your self-talk.

> Reflecting back what you are hearing, this helps with understanding.

Remember the gap. Refer to the comments in chapter three. Reflecting back helps us bridge the gap between what is said and what is understood. The phrase "What I heard you say is ..." is very helpful.

Eight: Be open to discovering more about yourself and the other person. You are not perfect. Grasping this with openness will enable you to hear more clearly or maybe even for the first time.

Nine: Become aware of your body language and

tone. Note what you say without speaking. Examples are: slouching back, arms folded, legs curled back, rolling eyes, interrupting, looking away, escalating voice volume, increasing voice tone, shortness of breath. On the positive side are: leaning in, eye contact, open arms, proper regular breathing, a steady voice, skin contact, and body touch to mention a few.

Ten: Become aware of triggers. 'My mama always told me' might work for Forest Gump but can be a trigger for your spouse, especially when it comes to her cooking. These landmines can go off unexpectedly. Sometimes you will hit them inadvertently but to do it again, purposefully, is just stupid. Make a note of obvious ones for future reference. As a general note, most men will react when they feel exposed or disrespected, and most women when feeling unloved or afraid.

> Eventually, every comment results in an explosion.

What if it is done wrong?

The consequences of conflict handled poorly, or not well, can be devastating and destroying. This is an artform, and we all need to become masters. At the simplest level, conflict can cause damage to the other person that can take a lot of time to heal. Sometimes a lifetime. You're too stupid, ugly, fat, to get this, be this or do this, are some examples of approaches that could leave irreparable damage well after the heated conversation has concluded. This will only build barriers and block out future vulnerability and transparency. Effectively killing loving, meaningful communication, which is the lifeblood of any good relationship.

> The consequences of conflict handled badly can be life destroying and devastating.

I saw a great illustration using a piece of paper to represented a marriage. Each conflict not well-handled was like tearing a portion of the paper off. This left less safe space for conversation. For example, he brings up finances and she explodes. Finances are no longer something he will want to bring up. It is now removed, or torn away, as a safe topic. She brings up his time with his friends and he erupts. Eliminated from safe ground, the page gets smaller. You continue this kind of "communication" for a few years, and there will be very little left of the paper, no safe space for conversation. Eventually, every comment will result in an explosion. Have you been there? Are you there now?

When a couple cannot communicate about important issues without fighting, their union develops into what is called a 'Railroad Marriage.' Both parties keep up the facade of marriage held together by kids and other responsibilities, much like the sleepers that hold the train tracks together. This continues until those are no longer a factor, then they split apart. This explains why you see people in their 40 and 50's getting divorced. (which remember, is supposed to be the glorious expression of the community of God). You wonder why after 30 years, or more, of marriage they call it quits! In reality, they separated years ago, the only difference is now it's public.

Divorce is the beginning of hell. The 'D' word is banned in our house and is very, very rarely the answer. More about that later.

CONFLICT

Counseling

Counseling is an excellent option for any couple that wants to grow closer together. We have lost the value and input from the Grampas and the Nanas. Back in the day, when the family was indeed a cohesive unit, those conversations around the dinner table would be seasoned with words of wisdom. Young people and new marriages could do to hear from those who are mature in life and love. In the relaxed format of laughs and lunch, there was much learning. Unfortunately we have lost our Elders input and mentoring in the business and disconnectedness of the national and international family. So we need local counselors. The stigma attached to seeking outside help thankfully is waning. The advantage of a third person's perspective cannot be overstated, especially when you are stuck in a stalemate. Discovering what is 'normal,' and what is not, can be very liberating and uniting to a couple. You may not be as messed up as you think.

What happens when conflict is done right?

There is understanding, there is growth, there is a connection. With understanding one another, there can come a change in attitude and new learning. We have had an excellent chance to see ourselves through someone else's eyes. This might not be as pretty as we would like, but it is real and needs to be viewed. The new unity brings vigor and excitement to what is possible. This refreshed attitude will cause deposits and investments in each other's emotional bank accounts. Conflict done

> **Done well, a good conflict can result in a win-win feel that can translate into emotional love deposits.**

badly makes withdrawals. Forgiveness and reconciliation switch toxicity out and draw love into your relational atmosphere! Done well, a good conflict can result in a win-win feel that can translate into emotional love deposits (this can feel like some of those moments when you first met). Love deposits are crucial because when a love tank runs dry, it is exceedingly difficult to get the engine turning over again.

Speed Notes on Chapter 4

- Husbands and wives fight, *and so we should!* Or we could say, disagree strongly?
- **Conflict** the fourth conversation, is God's way of helping us see ourselves because we always bring ourselves to every fight. "What did I say or do that hurt you? I am sorry I do not understand?"
- When you blow a conflict, and we will, you always have the opportunity to apologize and head back and start again.
- Attack the problem not the person.
- Real men and strong ladies will not leave an argument or conflict from being resolved. Move in gently.
- Be aware of the context, has he just walked in? Is she exhausted?
- Do not generalize deal with one topic at a time. Use 'I' language.
- One will be quick with words, the other full of regrets, be patient with each other.
- If s/he is *not* looking at you, you do not have their undivided attention.
- Use CONFLICT CONVERSATIONS (on following pages).

Action Steps

- Have a private date and lean gently into a topic of conflict. Use the Conflict Conversation Cheat Sheet at the end of the chapter. Focus on the other person. Prioritize understanding and unpacking. Peel back the layers of dialogue to discover what the underlying emotions, feelings, and thoughts are. Be a relational adventurer. Remember it is not about you! Be nice!
- Have a conversation about a mentoring couple or a counselor that you will both meet with on a regular basis. Gramps and Grandma might be an option.
- Develop a shared calendar, that both can access. Plan to block out some weekly time to remain on the same page with the family schedule. This will do a lot in heading off some conflict and help with communicating. We find on hour on a Sunday night works well for us.
- Exercise the spiritual discipline of *Meditation*.

CONFLICT

Conflict Conversation Cheat Sheet

Now lean into a conflict: Use the layout. Here is a copy of it.

1. Begin with an affirmation - I love you because.
2. Dissect one problem at a time (Remember: The problem not the person!)
3. Use 'I feel' or 'I think' language.
4. One speaks, and the other actively listens.
5. Reflect back what you have heard.
6. Peel back the layers.
7. Get clarity.
8. Understand your role in the problem.
9. Brainstorm for solutions.
10. Come to an agreement and affirm each other.

    Do Not:

    Attack the other person

    Do:

    Discover and be curious about your spouse

In short, Build, Break, Build, or in our married language, Love, Stretch, Love!

ELEVEN C'S FOR A STRONG MARRIAGE

Some Typical 'Unsafe' Conversations

- I feel like I have to take all the spiritual responsibilities.
- I feel like I have to be responsible for most family stuff.
- I feel like I am the kid's taxi.
- I think our kids' are in too many activities.
- I am concerned that vacations are all on me.
- I am worried about our accommodations.
- It feels to me like I have to do all the chores.
- It appears that you have financial freedom, not me.
- I feel like I have to care for the pets.
- I feel like I have to fight technology for your attention.
- I am anxious to take a rest, as I think you disapprove.
- I am sometimes embarrassed by your public behavior.
- I am afraid when you drink.
- I am sure you are unaware, but there are times it seems like you are flirting. I get insecure when I do not have access to your phone.
- I'm afraid of the influence of some of your friendships.
- I feel lonely when you cannot take some time for me.
- There are times I feel neglected.
- I feel lost when your attention is elsewhere.
- I am hurt when you use harsh words with me.
- I'm confused when you don't use certain words.
- At times I do not feel loved.
- Sometimes I do not feel like a priority.
- I sometimes feel belittled by the way you speak to me.
- I am scared by the atmosphere you create around you.
- I feel invisible when you do not touch me.
- I feel lonely when you use your energy/time with others.
- I don't feel appealing when you don't comment on me.
- I do not feel successful when you do not mention my hard work or success.

CHAPTER 5

Common Vision

"Where there is no vision, the people perish"

Chapter 5

Common Vision

A Conversation about The Target

Zig Ziglar said "If you aim at nothing you will hit it every time." A couple heading into marriage without having had a conversation about **Common Vision** is like taking aim at an absent target.

Rod's Story: I see things a little differently at times. We were serving God in the small country church in Mpumalanga, South Africa, when we confirmed the call and decision to move to the USA. I merely said, "Cheryl, we will board a plane and the rest will be easy."

We had just agreed to the macro plan of a 3-year mission adventure. What I had not considered was relocating a toddler, fitting our lives into six suitcases, liquidating two vehicles, rent management for our apartment, organizing transport and communication resources for the States, etc. Cheryl, on the other hand, thought of all of this. So when I said, "Hey Honey, I agreed to be there in six weeks!" She lost it! She said, "You want me to leave everything I have worked for, including wedding gifts, baby shower treasures, mementos, and keepsakes. You want me to leave family, friends, and all that is familiar. You want me to move from the sunny shores of Port Elizabeth to the harsh winters of the Michigan climate?"

Bearing in mind we actually lived right on the beachfront. Literally, you walked across a street, and you were standing on the soft white sands of the Indian Ocean. I mean dolphins in the waves, seagulls and surf, kind of ocean.

"You want me to hold my studies, care for our kid, say goodbye to my parents and family, and get on a plane in six weeks!"

Apparently, I was not thinking of the common vision for my family. I received the rebuke, but we left in six weeks anyway. Now looking back, that was 20 years ago!

Our Church recently encouraged us to create a family vision statement. A statement of focus that is designed to include all the values you believe is important. A vision statement is a little like a family budget. Once you have decided what is important, it is easy to eliminate things that do not size up with those values. So for example, we believe Church is fundamental, it does not become an every Sunday tug-of-war. There are no conversations about who is going and why. It is just part of who we are and what we do. No need for conflict.

A good vision statement will guide the future. The values that are embedded in this statement will also shape the next few generations. Just dream what it is like to create a standard for your children's children.

Some family vision statements are simple, some are acrostic, some are rather long, some are measurable. Begin with the essential elements then try to be creative in how you put them together.

> **A good vision statement will guide the future.**

For Example:

Let's say you have these 5 key elements or values in your family:
1. Faith in God,
2. Respect for one another,

3. Life-long learning
4. Healthy living,
5. Fun

It might look something like:

"The Sanderson-Smith family will honor God first and foremost, we will respect each other, and strive to be lifelong learners. We will aspire to healthy living and in all our striving will make fun a hallmark of being one of us."

(Memory version: "We will honor God, respect each other, love learning, live healthily and be a fun-filled family.")

Story: We just bought a new house. We had saved $3500 for a new pool and discovered that we actually needed a new roof. Practical me said we need a new roof. Fun wife said we need a new pool. She said, "Well if the roof leaks we get an indoor pool out of the deal." So patch the roof, put in the pool? You can guess what we did! Happy wife happy life!

The key to a united vision is to work it out, fine tune it, and write it down. Make it simple, make it easy to remember. Most of all, include elements and values that you would like your children's children to remember.

What we found interesting was the migration of ideas that we had taken from the vision of our parents. These instilled, intentionally or unintentionally, resonated from deep within us. This is the critical place to ask God for discernment about what values and ideas should be kept and what should be elimi-

> **Work it out, fine tune it and write it down.**

nated, even though it all feels so right.

Scripture puts it like this in Proverbs 29:18:

> *"Where there is no vision, the people perish"* [1]

Once we formulated our values and passions, we talked about some nuts and bolts. This might seem easy, but we had just as much 'strong interaction' over these as well. For example once you have decided God is important and maybe so is fun, you have to determine if you are going to live the American dream (white picket fence and 2.5 kids) or travel the world. Chew on it, work it through. Are you buying a house in the country or in the suburbs? Are you going to remain debt-free, so purchase something small and remodel up? Are you going to have dogs or cats? Are you going to have a ranch, loft or Dad's basement? (There is a conversation resource at the end of the chapter to help you tease out your thoughts).

> **What is your dream? What is your vision?**

Story: When we had just returned from our three-day honeymoon we told you about, I thought being very frugal meant organizing to move into our neighbor's granny flat. This was a small unit next to the main house, for cheap rent. At about 6 am the 'caring' neighbor knocked on our window. We were woken up from a 'newly-wed' embrace, with coffee and a neighborly desire for active conversation. Needless to say, my new bride insisted we move within the week. We did!

Are you going to have a soccer Mom van or a two-seater sports car? These are just some questions that will guide you into a more significant and more in-depth understanding of the person you are about to spend your life with! Common vision is more about being on the same page with the same vision, than clones. Compatibility and resonance will result.

You may, of course, have it all planned out, the truth is, life is fluid and change is constant so be ready for tweaks along the way. Ok, honestly those tweaks can be significant life altering events. Then its back to recalibrate.

Just a quick sidebar before we get too far. Talking about compatibility, there is no such thing as being sexually *in*compatible. You are sexually compatible. It is designed to work and work just right, so no need to explore that until the wedding day.

Brett Salkeld, the co-author of 'How Far Can We Go? A Catholic Guide to Sex and Dating' puts it like this:

> There is no such thing as sexual *IN*compatibility.

"In fact, though cohabitation looks a lot like marriage on the surface, it is missing the very heart of marriage, namely a promise to be faithful come what may. And without this promise, cohabitation ends up being not a close analogate of marriage, but its radical opposite. While marriage says, "I'll be with you no matter what," cohabitation says, "I'll be with you as long as I can stand you." It says, "If you do your share of the housework, and pay your share of the bills, and keep me satisfied sexually, I'll stick around. But if you don't, well, I guess it wasn't meant to be." The natural God given desire for physical intimacy should serve to help us focus on the other aspects of our relationship where our urge to serve the other person is compromised by human weakness. Foreplay starts with helping around the house and listening when someone has had a bad day. When "sexual compatibility" becomes something independent of relational compatibility as a whole, sex becomes less and less capable of confirming and sealing the commitment between two people who have promised their lives to one another. And when we strip sex of its power to hold people together by isolating it from its normal role in a relationship, we should not be surprised when marital breakdown follows."

Broadly, compatibility is not about being clones or altering the other person into your likeness. It is the conversation of what happens when we have a different set of priorities or varying perspectives.

Action: Separately complete and rate the following 12 themes in order of priority (the first being most important to the least): Money, Career, Children, Family, Fun, Work, Sex, Stuff, Friends, God, Church, and Christian Community (There is a list at the end of the chapter for you to work through). Do not discuss these until each of you has completed your own personal ordered list.

Now come together and compare your answers with each other. Where there are similarities celebrate and high five. Where there are significant discrepancies spend some time having the conversation

> Broadly, compatibility is not about being clones or altering the other person into your likeness. It is the conversation of what happens when we have a different set of priorities.

about what this means for each of you. Treat each other with respect and love and make sure not to dismiss or devalue the other person's priority list. Remember you have learned how to communicate and you have even learned how to have a conflict. Use your new skills. Be gentle with each other. This is a level of intimacy that very few even venture into, and can scary and uncomfortable. Note some areas seem to align at first might not actually after further exploration and discussion of your understanding of the topics or values.

Say for example you both identify Career is your number four pick. What does that mean? Does that mean you will be dedicating hours a week to developing your career path? Maybe you will be looking to move from job to job for corporate development? Could that mean you would want to even move to another city? The other person might value work stability and seek to keep a job and retire there with a 30-year plan. So it is important to unpack your choices and explain your intentions.

Cheryl's Story: Things change; we each had three jobs. I was planning on being a career mom. I worked at a local bank and was always the first in and last staff member out. I carried a branch key and would be the on-call person for many weekends. I was loved and given a lot of responsibility, respect, authority and was well remunerated for it. I was on an upward, onward, corporate ladder climb that was tracking exponentially.

After maternity leave, my boss welcomed me back with open arms, the next second I unexpectedly burst into tears! I resigned immediately and became a full-time mom.

This is not for everyone, but be ready for the unexpected and the life changes when they hit. Learn to be flexible and to embrace change and movement.

We are one

> You have decided to get married so everything is a team effort from now on. This is important.

We decided to get married! From now on everything becomes a team effort. We are one.

Rod's Story: I remember the night Cheryl said she was done with me! I remember it so distinctly. It was a Sunday night during the 6:30 evening worship service and we were serving as the youth pastoral team of Walmer Methodist Church at the time.

She leaned over to me and just said "Rod I am done! I am no longer fighting for attention, fighting for priority, fighting to be loved, fighting to be cherished. I am done. I am done."

The words were not loud, not angry, just filled with a sense of resignation. They hit me like a ton of bricks, penetrating, as I thought we had a decent marriage with all its usual dynamics, but good none the less.

I remember heading down to the altar in tears. One of my best friends and members of our small group Bible study, Ray, came down with me. We prayed, cried and prayed again. I asked God to help me! I did not know how to love this woman. I did not know how to make her a priority. I did not see my self-consumption and childlike behavior. I did not notice that we were still two single people sharing a house and responsibilities. Through tears and pain, I began to see that we were not closer, not united and certainly not becoming one.

This began a lifelong decision and determination to discover how to love her. How to be fully married. How to enjoy God's plan and ultimately the motivation and content for this book.

This is an important transition. You had or have an opportunity to be single. You had a choice to raise your hands when the DJ said 'and all the single ladies, get your hands up.' You had time to jump out of airplanes, bungee jump the Bloukrans gorge, take selfies on radio towers, parkour on top of buildings, and take snacks from pregnant moms. But now you are deciding to be married. You put away single things, you move towards the one you love. This maturing is referred to by the apostle Paul in 1 Corinthians 13:11:

> 'When I was a child, I talked like a child, I thought like a child, I reasoned like a child. When I became a man, I put the ways of childhood behind me.'

We are excited for you, but here is the clincher. Life is now different. You now are a unit, a team. You are far more concerned with your spouse's needs and wants than your own. The Bible puts it like this in Ephesians 5 verse 25-28:

> "Husbands, love your wives, just as Christ loved the church and gave himself up for her (Died) to make her holy, cleansing her by the washing with water through the word, and to present her to himself as a radiant church, without stain or wrinkle or any other blemish, but holy and blameless. In this same way, husbands ought to love their wives as their own bodies. He who loves his wife loves himself."

> **"Husbands, love your wives, just as Christ loved the church and gave himself up for her".** Can you imagine if every marriage felt like this?

Can you imagine if every marriage felt like this? What would it be like if you saw all men sacrificing their own agendas, options, desires for the one they love? How different would the divorce rate be if this was the new normal?

Instead, we have a lot of boys out there masquerading in men's bodies, consumed with themselves and their own agendas. They are waiting longer and longer to get married because it is all about them. After a late night of party and games, the 20 or 30-year-olds return home like a rebellious teenager to apologize to the 'Ball and Chain' for being out so late with his or her friends.

This highly narcissistic culture is placing two childish, self-consumed individuals together in the act of marriage and wondering why they are not making it. God says in Scripture that challenges and hardships bring maturity, yet we instead aim to remove all the struggle from our children[2]. They remain childlike and self-consumed and are shocked by the discovery that another human is not there to meet their every need. The fact that this other person might actually have some thoughts, needs, and desires that are different from theirs, go figure!

Does this mean all boys nights or girls nights are out of bounds? No, but they should undoubtedly happen with less frequency. Venues where young boys are on the hunt for young girls, and they make themselves desirable for the pursuit. Atmospheres charged with attraction and lust is not necessarily optimum for the married couple. Our new environment should be

> A mature couple or person, in the faith, and married will help you discern if you are being selfish or you are embracing every part of your specific God-given gender.

different. It should feel different. Adults behave differently[3]. In fact, if you do not begin to migrate to having more fun with your beautiful or amazing choice, there might be some issues with your decision or your maturity. Your person is about to say 'I do' to a lifetime with you deserves to feel top of your list, under God of course.

A married mentor will help you with perspective. There are times when men have to go out, build something, hunt something, break something and eat something. Additionally there are times when girls should buy something, talk about something, and again talk about something or eat chocolate. So perspective is key. A mature faith-filled married couple will help you discern if you are being selfish or are embracing every part of your specific God-given gender.

Annual Plan

Inviting your man or woman to consider an annual plan for a healthy marriage is a golden idea. Sadly, us boys are hard wired to conquer. Unfortunately once we get the girl, we can often forget a beautiful flower needs consistent love and attention. Just like I did.

An annual plan may consist of weekly dates, monthly moments and possibly several planned yearly activities that you do together to enrich your marriage.

Remember we put more time and effort into baking a chocolate cake than planning ingredients for our marriage. A Christian financial course, something on parenting, a love-each-other-more retreat, or a course on love languages are great

> An annual plan consists of several planned activities that you would do together to enrich your marriage.

examples of activities that could be part of this plan.

Childhood Template

Your story, or history, is your childhood template. This strongly shape your compatibility and values. You have learned how to behave and observed values, good and bad from the day your Mom popped you out. Some of these will resonate with your new spouse, some will clash. Discuss with your spouse the situations, words, and stories that shaped you, and them, as children. Have a conversation about how and where you each learn and developed your separate worldviews.

> Your compatibility and your values will come very strongly from your story, your childhood template.

Cheryl's Story: Punctuality was essential to my family. My parents didn't drive due to horrific vehicle accidents when they were kids, so keeping our 'uber' waiting was unheard of. We would have to be ready 20 or 30 minutes before pickup time. We would sit patiently in our living room waiting for our ride with bags and jackets on.

Rod's family were always running from one thing to another, being on time was a struggle. The first time I was invited to a day of swimming and water skiing with them, they had planned to leave at 6.30 am. I packed the night before and left my home with time to spare as not to keep them waiting. I arrived at a sleeping house, so departure time ended up being more like 8.30ish. Different templates, different values. Today Rod still says we can pack five minutes of action into a 4-minute time slot.

ELEVEN C'S FOR A STRONG MARRIAGE

United we stand

An orchestra is made up of many individuals and, although each is beautiful in their own right, they sound so much better together. This is Divine math. One plus one equals three. The integrated approach to marriage will bring out more and better, than the sum of the two individuals. This interdependence is not unhealthy. We need each other.

> **The united approach to marriage will bring out more than the sum of the two individuals.**

Can single people be whole, complete? Of course! But is there something unique in a marriage? Absolutely! True unity takes time and work.

Cheryl's Story: Our older children have very fond memories of being the only two nieces. Before my brother, Rob found his wonderful wife Elaina, they were spoiled. They got to have uncle date nights, shopping sprees, expensive coffee shop experiences, late-night shenanigans, midnight ice cream socials, and getting hard cash for swimming laps, giving back massages and cleaning their teeth. They got something their parents could not afford. Time! Single people were gold in their lives. Fast forward, add a marriage and three rugrats and our girls feel robbed! For some reason, his wife and kids have become a higher priority.

Activity: Take a moment right now, if you can, to put your head to their chest and listen. Guys focus, I know what you are thinking! Listen to their loves and dreams. Hear their visions and values. Remember Jesus died for this amazing resonating heart!

So How?

First: Pray. Ask God to guide and empower you to hear His voice as you define the reason you exist as a team. God has a vision for you as a person and as a couple. You are all you need to be. You are at the place you need to be. You are everything you need to be. You are here for what God wants.

Second: The questions you ask will reveal the answers you get. That might sound ridiculously obvious, but Common Vision all revolves around the outcomes you want to achieve as a couple. Questions like:

- What atmosphere do we want to generate in our home?
- What do we want future generations to remember about us?
- What is the legacy we want to be remembered for?
- Where are we going to invest our time?
- What are some important things for us?
- What are essential cornerstones of our lives?
- What are some values that you want to hold high?
- What is our purpose?
- What should it be like being married to each of us?
- What will our budget and calendar say about us?
- What value will we bring to future generations?

Third: Write all the responses down. Do not criticize. Do not evaluate. Do not edit. Do not clip or crop. Just attempt to listen well and capture thoughts and feelings.

Fourth: Take all these ideas and distill them into a few clear, consensus-driven statements. They do not have to be pretty or rhyme. The critical thing is they are captured.

Fifth: Now summarize and celebrate: Wordsmith them into a more logical, linear and presentable Common Vision statement.

Display it for all to see and remember.

Speed Notes on Chapter 5

- A Common Vision statement guides the future.
- It is designed to include all the values that you believe are important, a little like a family budget.
- Write down all your ideas, unfiltered.
- Your vision statement will be influenced by your history and context, become aware.
- Use the resources at the end of this chapter to discover your spouse's dreams and desires.
- You are sexually compatible, take my word for it, this does not have to be tested. God made it that way.
- Compatibility does not mean being a clone. It means seeking a common vision and hearing the heart of the one you love.
- This will unite you as you move forward. Remember that marriage is about maturing, not being a boy or girl living out selfishness.
- Desire annual input, in many forms, to continue to grow through your marriage for, say the next 50 years.
- Build and write out a family Common Vision Statement. It will take time and dedication, but do not get weak on this. It will set the target. Make it simple, make it easy to remember but most of all include elements and values that you would like your children's children to remember.

Action Steps

- Have a private date and cut out time to discuss your Common Vision. Bring along your book so you can use the work pages at the end of the chapter. This might take more than one date. Let the process develop organically. Listen and reflect. Dig deep to understand. This will bring you closer than all the hugs and kisses. Write out the Common Vision Statement.
- Here is your next date plan. Find one of those do it yourself sign companies or activate your arts and crafts skills, and create your Common Vision statement plaque. Place it somewhere that you can see it daily as a reminder.
- Take out your calendar and mark the next 2 or 3 annual events that you would like to do to impact your marriage. Eg. Look up the next 'Laugh Your Way to a Better Marriage[4]' live event near you or a 'Financial Peace Course[5]'.
- Exercise the spiritual discipline of *Fasting*.

You will each need a copy of this list. You do not want to see each other's numbers until you are done. Go down the list and mark the most important as 1, the next as 2 and so on. Once you are all done, compare with each other.

Compatibility

		Boy	Girl
God	Your spiritual formation, taking time on a daily basis to grow in your relationship with God.		
Money	Your dedication to making money, becoming debt free, taking on extra jobs, saving and giving.		
Career	Your dedication to your career, looking for growth and movement opportunities by adding study programs for progress.		
Family	Your dedication to your family, dads, and moms on both sides. All siblings. Family gatherings, family events.		
Fun	Your commitment to fun, recreation, taking the initiative, facilitating, making fun a part of what you do.		
Sex	Your commitment to the intimate connection between each other.		

ELEVEN C'S FOR A STRONG MARRIAGE

		Boy	Girl
Friends	Your commitment to your friends, your past ones, your new ones, your married ones, your single ones.		
Children	Your commitment to having children, investing in them, caring for them.		
Community	Your commitment to a Christian community, investing in others and having others invest in you. A weekly commitment.		
Work	Your commitment to moving up the corporate ladder. If it's a move in town or out of town, in state or out of state, creating job growth opportunities.		
Church	You commitment to a place of Spiritual formation and worship on a regular basis.		
Stuff	Things. Goodies. Toys. The things we gather.		
Experiences	Travel, journey, learn, discover, develop. Adventures to the unknown.		

COMMON VISION

Circle what you think your spouse will want? Do they want to live in the country or the city? How many boy children and/or girl children does s/he want? When you're each done, compare your lists.

Common Vision Exploration

His List

Live:	Country	City
Children:	Boys #	Girls #
Pets:	Dogs #	Cats #
Transport:	Van #	Car #
	Truck #	Bicycle #
Type of Home:	Apartment	House
	Garages #	
	Bedrooms #	Bathrooms #
Vacation:	Beach	Mountain
	Internationally	Locally

ELEVEN C'S FOR A STRONG MARRIAGE

Her List

Live:	Country	City
Children:	Boys #	Girls #
Pets:	Dogs #	Cats #
Transport:	Van #	Car #
	Truck #	Bicycle #
Type of Home:	Apartment	House
	Garages #	
	Bedrooms #	Bathrooms #
Vacation:	Beach	Mountain
	Internationally	Locally

CHAPTER 6

Captains

These are men who are dedicated to the common vision and are leading with a servant heart towards a common goal with a gentle, yet firm tenacity to reach for the dreams of their beautiful bride and expanding family.

Chapter 6

Captain

A Conversation about Who's in Charge?

If there are too many followers or too many leaders chaos ensues. Who leads in what areas is our next conversation called **Captains**.

> If there are too many followers or too many leaders chaos ensues.

Story: On a bright sunny day on September 11th, 2001 numerous terrorists launched an attack on America. They hijacked four commercial airlines packed full of passengers and flew them maliciously into The World Trade Center and the Pentagon. The fourth flight attack was thwarted by brave and heroic civilians that forced it to abandon the mission and crash into the fields of Pennsylvania.

8:46 am the first plane struck the World Trade Center North Tower. The second flies into the South Tower at 9:03 am. A third hit the Pentagon at 9:37 am. We can remember where we were that day. A regular day at the office, housekeeping, cooking, and then life stopped. I remember running to Cheryl and alerting her. The world seemed to stand still, watching in disbelief, frozen in shock. In the meantime, without hesitation, hundreds of First Responders rushed towards the chaos and pain. Burning and blistering airplane fuel, smoldering buildings, and dust covered people did not scare them.

One of the biggest hindrances to successful life-saving operations was the lack of an immediate central command and a common language. All first responders departments that were rushing to Ground Zero were focused on one thing: saving lives. An immediate well coordinated effort was needed. A terrorist attack of this magnitude had never happened before on US soil. There was no space for error. However disaster happened that day, the bloody and grey images still plague our minds. The sights and sounds burned into our thoughts as we all witnessed 2996 people die. This included 411 caring and committed police, firefighters, ambulance, and medical personnel.

There were too many chiefs. It was virtually impossible to make a clear, concise and calculated decision when some leaders were saying go and others were saying no. Not all of them could see the bigger picture. Good leadership saves lives *and* marriages.

> **Marriage is designed by God with a structure.**

Cheryl is a first born and likes to be in charge. I am a first born and like to be in charge! Marriage is designed by God with a structure. This is evident in the roles and responsibilities drawn out in Genesis 1 - 3 and then echoed throughout Scripture.

Is leading worth a higher status than following? This is an important question to answer because the struggle for power in life, partnerships, and marriage can be divisive. How did it happen that 'leader' is considered more and 'follower' less? The answer lies in lousy leadership. True leadership is sacrificial. If this is true, then which is more desirable: to lead sacrificially or to follow faithfully?

Cheryl's Story: I teach at an elementary school. One day one of the kindergartner's said, "I think Emlyn's Dad, likes you!" Emlyn is our third born. Good to know because after 27 years of marriage it can still be seen from the outside. One of the kids then asked "Why does he bring you coffee?" I said "I think he just wants a smooch!" Needless to say, you can imagine the response. But many days, Rod will bring me a coffee, not because he has to, but because he wants to. Serving one another is fun, and at times, there are lovely rewards. More about that in Chapter 10.

    Modern western culture places a higher value on leadership than on good 'followership,' (if I can build a new word here). There are many leadership conferences but not much 'followership' training. The program could include a celebration of dedication, the meaning of commitment, how to serve under healthy authority, tools to resist eroding gossip, what is communication from the trenches, ways to celebrate people's unique gifts, to list just a few. I have often thought of putting together a conference like that but I am afraid that it would not succeed. Western society does not seem to celebrate the advantages of rank and file or the contented team member.

    The Bible is clear in Genesis that men and women are created in His image. That means that both Cheryl and I have a God deposit within us, a God fingerprint on us, a God reflection from us, and a God form and shape. No other part of creation was made in *God's image*. Each reflect God in unique ways. Each has equal value. Genesis 1 verse 27 says:

> "So God created mankind in his own image, in the image of God he created them; male and female he created them."

    This means that no matter what roles each gender plays, they both have equal *value*.

> **This means that no matter what roles each gender plays they both have equal value. But different roles.**

Leadership is then a function, not a status.

Moreover, the leadership function primarily aims to serve. Unfortunately, ego driven and fear mongering leaders have developed massive followings. Fear has been franchised to create huge impact. Power is addicting. Adam and Eve wanted control. Sin thrives on rebellion and misdirected power.

Jesus shattered these preconceived ideas on leadership. In His day, a leader was the most affluent, the strongest, the one with the most significant power. He demonstrated what REAL leadership looks like. He showed servant leadership. This must not be forgotten or underplayed, because abuse of power by anybody is not God's will and unacceptable. But neither is abdication and passivity.

> **Jesus demonstrated what real leadership looked like, he showed servant leadership.**

Ephesians 5 verse 21 to 33 speaks of the importance of mutual submission in marriage. From both the man and the woman and the requirements of a man to love a woman as he does his own body. (Men, just think for a moment how much you do actually love your body? Gym time, cleaning time, mirror time etc.) This sort of love and leadership is sacrificial and complimentary. Let's look at the apostle Paul, a biblical character who had a dramatic God-encounter. This is written about in the New Testament. He went on to write letters to the Ephesians:

> *"Submit to one another out of reverence for Christ. Wives, submit yourselves to your own husbands as you do to the Lord. For the husband is the head of the wife as Christ*

> **This sort of love and leadership is sacrificial and complimentary.**

is the head of the church, his body, of which he is the Savior. Now as the church submits to Christ, so also wives should submit to their husbands in everything. Husbands, love your wives, just as Christ loved the church and gave himself up for her to make her holy, cleansing her by the washing with water through the word, and to present her to himself as a radiant church, without stain or wrinkle or any other blemish, but holy and blameless. In this same way, husbands ought to love their wives as their own bodies. He who loves his wife loves himself. After all, no one ever hated their own body, but they feed and care for their body, just as Christ does the church for we are members of his body. "For this reason a man will leave his father and mother and be united to his wife, and the two will become one flesh." This is a profound mystery but I am talking about Christ and the church. However, each one of you also must love his wife as he loves himself, and the wife must respect her husband."

I believe that the reason he enters into the conversation speaking first to wives, is because of Genesis 3 verse 6:

"To the woman he said, "I will make your pains in childbearing very severe; with painful labor you will give birth to children. Your desire will be for your husband, and he will rule over you."

"*This desire for your husband,*" we do not believe is a desire only for him physically, but primarily a desire for his *role*. There will be a *sinful* desire inside Cheryl, that will cause her to desire to take leadership in our home, and even absorb the roles designed for me. That is why it is linked to the next

> Women will find a desire to take the leadership role in the home.

part of the sentence, 'he will rule over you.' The original audience of Genesis would have understood that being born first would automatically bring a different role to Adam. That is why Paul is calling women to that place of submission, hopefully, under Godly masculine leadership. A wise man will not yell this out in a conflict!

Men were designed and built to lead. God gave men the responsibility to name the animals and bring order in the garden of Eden (Genesis 2 verse 15 and 19). This leadership mandate continues. They are hard-wired to move into chaos and bring order (as in the garden), and they are made to define and name what they see (naming the animals).

> Men are supposed to 'lean in' and bring order out of chaos in their home, life and marriages.

The way this plays out in a marriage is that men are supposed to 'lean in' and bring order out of chaos in their homes, lives, and marriages. I confess I am not good at this. I tell men that if there is chaos in their lives, it is primarily their fault. They really do not like to hear that, neither do I, but it is true. If things are bad, real men do something about it.

No movement = no man. When men do not do the *next right thing*! When men are paralyzed by fear and feel incapable, they feel nothing like men.

This causes them to react like boys.

The man reverts back to the little son of his father. He does not step up and become a man, in his own right. In this leadership vacuum, women will be forced to step up and lead, *out of fear*. This is not in her natural design.

Rod's Story: I am a volunteer firefighter. This might

be me playing out some boyhood dream in and of itself. The fire alarms go off and the team responds. It can be anything from cat stuck in a tree, to a fully engulfed multistory apartment fire. The trucks roll, the firefighters gear up on route, placing on personal protective equipment, masks and tanks. As the trucks pull up, the trained rescuers, move into action. Adrenaline is only controlled by discipline and training. The sights, sounds and smells are typical. The emotions expected. Timing is crucial, and synergy and strategy save lives. We return, tired but feeling successful, like superheroes. A travesty was averted, we looked danger in the face, lives were saved.

Then I get home! Hero feelings quickly evaporate. Life can be tough. Add marriage, a few kids, and I can often feel overwhelmed. I feel 'incapable' of bringing order out of the insanity that is my home and life. Feelings of fear and shame arise. I react and begin to act out my childish behavior. I hit Kryptonite. Long lost are my superman thoughts, so I am stunned into silence and inactivity. So I clean the garage or mow the lawn, yet again. This does not form the safe structure Cheryl is needing.

Women are designed to fill this ordered structure, that is facilitated by the male. The female has the complementary role of filling the family structure with love and reflecting God's presence in her uniquely feminine way. However, when this does not happen, women will be forced to compensate. She will be filled with fear and insecurity. Her safety and that of their children are at risk. She will present as a

> Women are designed to fill this ordered structure, that is facilitated by the male, with the complementary role of filling it with love and reflecting God's presence.

progressively colder and more demanding woman. Developing a 'sharp edge' that will cause a growing apprehension in the man. The conversations will become more and more aggressive, and her tongue will become more attacking. The man will retreat further into his painful insecure world, and this will create a more substantial vacuum of leadership. The wife will then take further control and the destructive cycle continues.

One of the reasons that marriages are collapsing is the lack of a father leadership role-model for young men. In marriage, when things get tough, childlike boys bail and leave a trail of destruction behind them. They will run to a place they feel some masculine energy. Leadership is important. Godly masculine leadership is fundamental for the health of the family.

> This is a man that is dedicated to the common vision and is leading with a servant's heart towards a common goal with a gentle, yet firm tenacity to reach for the dreams of his beautiful bride and expanding family.

Masculinity under attack

Masculinity itself, however, is under attack. The growing trend towards gender fluidity, and a widening gender spectrum is making the celebration of maleness in any form, 'apparently' culturally insensitive. Even being called a man or a woman is in great debate. Some places of education and higher learning are now insisting on completely gender-neutral terms. This will become the norm. This is a tough and confusing world to grow up in. The strong chiseled man that goes forth to conquer the world on behalf of his family, taking decisive action in faith, to bring home the bacon and Godly order to their world is, sadly, becoming extinct.

Rod's Story: My parents spent hours teaching us ballroom dancing moves. To the classic sounds of Bach, we learned the Waltz, Foxtrot and Cha-cha. Cheryl invested hours in dance classes with ballet, tap and contemporary movement. We were extremely prepared for our senior prom. Men in tuxedos and ladies in full length evening gowns. The pomp, the circumstance, the dancing, the drama. They announced a couples competition. Cheryl, in her zeal, dragged me onto the floor. The chicken dance! Unfortunately, we won! First place chicken dance winners! Who wins a chicken dance? I really hope that did not make the yearbook.

For the sake of clarity; leadership is necessary for a dance, a marriage and in a home. Except for the chicken dance! I am supposed to lead as a servant leader, prepared to give my life for Cheryl. This servant leadership is not autocratic or dictatorial, but powerful and empowering. It is strong yet gentle. It is solid, yet pliable. It is masculine. It brings order out of chaos. It names the problems and consults for the conclusions. But it is necessary for a functioning happy home, without it, there will be casualties and even death.

The picture captured in the biblical vision of masculinity is a man who leads by sacrificing his agenda, his will, his way. He puts down his dreams, his aspirations and picks up the unified vision. He becomes its greatest champion.

What does this look like? This is a man that is dedicated to the common vision and is leading with a servant's heart towards a common goal with a gentle, yet firm tenacity to reach for the dreams of his beautiful bride and expanding family. Powerful preacher TD Jakes states it like this:

"No woman wants to be in submission to a man

who isn't in submission to God!"

There are places that women should lead within that structure. Some aspects and elements make far more sense for a woman to take the reins, to drive well and lead actively. Because her husband brings the primary leadership for the home does not mean that she has no leadership or exercises none. There are many areas where a wise husband will encourage and enlist the leadership skills of his wife, as part of his own leadership role.

> There are many areas where a wise husband will encourage and enlist the leadership call of his wife.

For example, my wife is working on her BPrimEd degree in Primary School education. She has far more knowledge than me on this subject and her more nurturing reflection of God, places her in the best position to lead concerning our own young daughter's schooling.

Rod's Story: As the festive season approaches each year, we go on our annual adventure, in anticipation of glistening lights and pine smells, for our living room. We call it the Great Christmas Tree Hunt!

There are however sometimes, when after a few hours of walking in the cold deep freezing snow, I would grab the closest Charlie Brown in reach and head for the hot chocolate. But this year we did particularly well. We found the perfect one, maybe a little larger than usual but a stellar green spruce all trimmed like the Rockefeller Center.

After dragging the show stopper home, we found that the base was too fat. It needed to be thinned to fit into the stand. No problem! I drag the tree to the basement and, being such a handyman, took out the circular saw. My goal: Cut a small piece off the side of the trunk. Challenge: I had no way to hold the tree still. I placed my sock covered foot on the trunk. Yep, you got it. The blade bit into the soft pine wood and ran up the tree right across my foot.

I felt it rip into flesh and without even looking, fell backwards, screaming. I yelled, "I cut off my foot, I cut off my foot!" I briefly heard people running as I drifted in and out of consciousness.

My fantastic wife ran downstairs calling the troops for Dads 'emergency'. She imagined looking for toes and grabbing ice. What she found was that in fact the blade had jumped over my foot, made the smallest little cut, more like a paper cut than an amputation. She got my youngest daughter to get me a booboo bandage, that had a Barbie on it! Her calm leadership under pressure and her sure and decisive handling of the situation brought calm to the hysterical patient.

In my defense, I really did think that I had lost a few digits, but the family does not let me live this one down.

In the end I did get the tree up, beautifully, that year!

Some healthy discussions as a couple are necessary. Each couple needs clarity about who is the captain of what. This is the place where order is constructed out of chaos. If every area needed a lengthy leadership debate, whenever there was a question or decision, we would get nowhere. If every area had no leadership, we would also get nowhere. So we take the time to have the necessary conversation.

> Each couple needs to get clarity about who is the captain of what. This is the place where order is constructed out of chaos.

No men

When men abdicate their leadership roles, we have a problem! This is a sure sign of a deeper masculine anomaly. In all probability he did not have a strong engaged masculine roll model. 'Man' was not spoken into his life as a young boy. He was not called up into his manhood, by other men, especially his father. Now he lives in fear of being incapable and exposed as such. He will need other men to stir that in him. This is the place for a men's small group.

His wonderful spouse could also use a small group of women. They could help her notice when she has filled the leadership vacuums in her home with the wrong spirit. They can help her rest in God's leadership provision through her man.

Mark Gungor illustrates a man's brain as working in boxes, one topic, one conversation at a time. While a woman's brain like spaghetti, everything connected, and all covered within one umbrella thought. This unique gender specific wiring means ladies will not typically, for example, forget a child behind. Men however can leave and lose their kids all the time. "Honey they were just here a second ago!" Men become so focused on the one-box project that world war three could break out, and he can be oblivious. It is not his lack of love or passion that the kids are screaming, the phone is ringing, the food is burning, and he is watching football. He is just in his football box and super-focused.

> **Men think in boxes, women think like spaghetti.**

Cheryl Story: I just have to mention that Rod has successfully lost each child at least once.

Tamryn was left at a youth group leader's house, and we got the 1 am call from them just wondering if we were close. Rod answered the phone attempting not to sound like he had just been woken and rushed there in his PJ's.

On a vacation adventure, sometime during the night, on a long road trip, Rod pulled into a rest stop for a much-needed bathroom break. Caylin and Emlyn jumped out and followed Rod in. He was quickly back behind the wheel, keen to make up the lost time when I awoke and asked him where the girls were. This strange and panicky look came over his face as he performed a police-style 180-degree turn and rushed back to get his girls. They were standing curbside, less than impressed. In his defense, he did not know the girls had followed him in. Boys!

This is one of the reasons that men have a high potential to lead with strength and clarity when all other stimuli around them demand their attention. They can lock in on one aspect, and once in focus, nothing can pull them out of it.

No leads

What happens when there are areas that nobody wants to lead?

There are areas that none of us wants to lead. These areas will take a particular sensitivity and dialogue to bring to a resolution. These should not be overlooked or ignored as they are a necessary part of doing life. An example might be keeping the house clean after both returns from a tiring day. Another example might be preparing and producing food.

A young couple might not be aware of all the areas that should be covered.

If areas are left unattended, especially important ones, like the budget, the house, the social calendar, etc. Very soon

> **There are areas that none of us wants to lead. These areas will take a special leadership sensitivity and dialogue to come to a resolution on.**

this home could regress into a blood bath of unfair accusations and threats. The resulting chaos might erupt and blessing will be lost in the depth of argument and tension.

'Followship' Styles

'Followship' Styles need also be noted. We have spoken a lot about leadership, but from the garden of Eden[4], humankind has had a problem with following. We will fight all our lives the pull of sin. Ultimate sin is our desire to be God. We are *always* going to struggle to resist the temptation to consider life from only our perspective. Think about how we feel about the temperature, our bank account, our work environment and how this other person does not fill all our needs! You are not alone. All humanity faces this dilemma. When we speak about faithful following, we find our sinful selves desiring to rebel.

> We will fight all our lives the pull of selfish sin. We want to be God!

Good followers recognize God has placed order and authority in place for a reason. He has the best in mind and therefore following His vision will bring the richest out of life.

Rod's Story: I cannot help but reach back to an earlier time in life. I was looking at an old classic picture sitting at the bedside of a hospice patient. The black and white is faded with age, the corners breaking down, the frame old and seasoned. But what had not lost any of its color was the look in the lady's eyes as she looked at her man in uniform, and his corresponding look and stance.

It was not a weak look of a woman with no power. No, this woman saw this man go to war. She held the house together, raised kids, for many years on her own, built a life, a family, a marriage. There was something so pure, so admirable, so rich within the look in her eyes. This was her man, and she was his woman. The pride in his face, the love in her hold. He chose her, and she felt chosen. He loved her and did whatever it took to provide a safe and secure home for her. She said yes and risked her life to spend her finite years on earth following him. He asked for her hand in marriage and spent his years discovering her.

Great followers inspire the best in others. They form great leaders by the words and ways they use to motivate, encourage and grow them. They look for an opportunity to see the best and facilitate the rest. Great followers make a healthy marriage, a beautiful family, an active Church, and a resonating community. In the words of 'A Million Dreams' from the Greatest Showman:

> **Great followers inspire the best in others.**

"However big, however small
Let me be part of it all
Share your dreams with me
You may be right, you may be wrong
But say that you'll bring me along
To the world you see
To the world I close my eyes to see
I close my eyes to see

Every night I lie in bed
The brightest colors fill my head
A million dreams are keeping me awake
A million dreams, a million dreams
I think of what the world could be

A vision of the one I see
A million dreams is all it's gonna take
A million dreams for the world we're gonna make
For the world we're gonna make ⁵"

Learning how to follow is learning how to see Jesus as our leader. Jesus says, come and follow me. Life is just an unpacking of that statement until you leave this earth. Followers of Jesus find it easier to follow other followers of Jesus.

In your marriage, follow Jesus and you will become a great leader. In your marriage, follow Jesus and you will become a great follower.

Remarried

Just a quick note to those who are getting remarried. This chapter is even more important to you.

When a man has destroyed his marriage or been widowed, his fear is heightened, and he becomes even more convinced that he is unable. He will be more guarded and could become more reactionary. Learning how to lead and follow well, will completely change his legacy.

A woman who has been through the pain of separation or divorce will be hurt and will react to situations with prejudice to defend and protect. She has been burned once before, deeply! She is now more tentative to allow herself to go there again. The very thought of following and falling within the safety of a man seems absurd and insane to her. Her journey to true freedom

> Men can react with heightened insecurity and ladies with heightened fear having been through the pain and devastation of divorce.

will come through true self-discovery and wise facilitation by her husband. For her learning to lead and follow appropriately will be an adventure peppered with possible hickups but brimming with potential liberation.

Speed Notes on Chapter 6

- Leadership or a **Captain** is necessary for a healthy marriage and leadership is part of God's structure for marriage.
- Men and women are created image bearers, in the image of God, and therefore have equal value but different roles and responsibilities.
- Great 'followership' is underrated but is just as important as great leadership, submission is not a swear word.
- There is a battle for leadership in the home. This began with Adam and Eve. Women will fight for his leadership role.
- Men who fear their capability to provide and lead, abdicate leadership and healthy movement. This could be detrimental to them and their family.
- A man that does not move into chaos is a man that has failed to bring his God-given strength and calling into his marriage and life. A man needs to do the next right thing!
- The biblical vision of masculinity is a man who leads by sacrificing his agenda, his will, his way for the common vision and good of his wife and family.
- Leadership is not controlling. Abdicated or absent leadership is just as bad. Leadership vacuums can cause disaster.
- A marriage that is sacrificially led will result in a dynamic team that will impact the generations to come. Who is the captain of what?

Action Steps

- Go to a local dance studio and sign up for ballroom dancing lessons. Learn how to lead and follow.
- Jump in the vehicle and head out for a day of Geocaching [6] but for the first half of the day let her drive and lead. Interact with one another and try to solve the clues. Now the second half of the day let him drive and lead. Have some great conversation about what worked and what did not. Speak about feelings and thoughts.
- Have a date and conversation about who led in what ways in your family of origin? Was Mom the matriarch, was Dad passive, was Dad a dictator, was Mom a doormat, how did that affect the way you entered into this conversation? How does that make you feel when it comes to leadership? Have you had a voice in the past? Did you lose your voice when you were younger? Now do you know what to do with this new vocal space?
- Write out a list of things that need to be well led in the running of a home, decide who is the primary leader of each area. E.g. Finances, Family Calendar, Spiritual formation, etc.
- Exercise the spiritual discipline of *Service.*

CHAPTER 7

Clan

God designed marriage as a safe place to expose your complete self. A private, personal, and intimate mirror for self-reflection from what you consider normal. You get to see yourself reflected back to you through the eyes of your spouse.

Chapter 7

Clan

A Conversation about the Tree you Marry.

Malcolm X, in *The Autobiography of Malcolm X* says:

"My feeling about in-laws was that they were outlaws."

Whether you like it or not, you marry into another whole family. This is the seventh conversation about the **Clan** or family.

Indeed, Author G.K. Chesterton, once wrote:

"Those nearest to our nearest may not happen to be the people who would have been our chief chosen friends, but they must be our friends; or memories are wounded and life made very ugly."

Take a moment to look at your future in-law family and take a second to consider this: *You marry them as well!* They will become a dominant affecting part of your entire life and marriage. You are about to adopt one of their clan into your family, by marrying one of their children. Bonus, you will also interact and engage with them for the rest of their lives. Scary, right!

> You marry your in-laws when you wed your wife.

Rod's Story: I can remember telling Cheryl it did not matter. It did not matter that we have vastly different upbringings, it did not matter our families had some contrasting values, it did not matter our priorities differed, perspectives differed, and well, even Sunday lunch differed. I remember saying to her, "Cheryl I am marrying you, and you are marrying me, nothing else matters."

I lied! There is nothing further from the truth. You marry the girl, and you get the grumpy Grampa in the deal! Yep you the winner.

Intergenerational Impact

The Bible is full of genealogies. These are celebrations of biological lineage. I often wondered why God placed such long and exhaustive lists in scripture, knowing that in the future an ADD guy like myself will just skim through them. He wanted us to remember and celebrate those that have gone before us. Because it is who we are. We are a unique combination and collaboration of all of our past influences. We follow in the genetic line of our parents and science has noted that we carry the mitochondrial DNA from our mothers. Science is calling its source, the first DNA, Eve[1].

The previous generation, especially, has a tremendous effect on who or what we become. We end up emulating many of the values, traits, and habits of our parents until you 'become' your Dad or Mom. If Dad had a coffee after dinner, the chances are you will feel a great urge to have a coffee after your meal. This is not a significant influence when it comes to coffee, but when it comes to other aspects of life, marriage, faith, and living, it can be exciting and complimentary or frightening and devastating.

> **We are a unique combination and collaboration of all of our past influences.**

ELEVEN C'S FOR A STRONG MARRIAGE

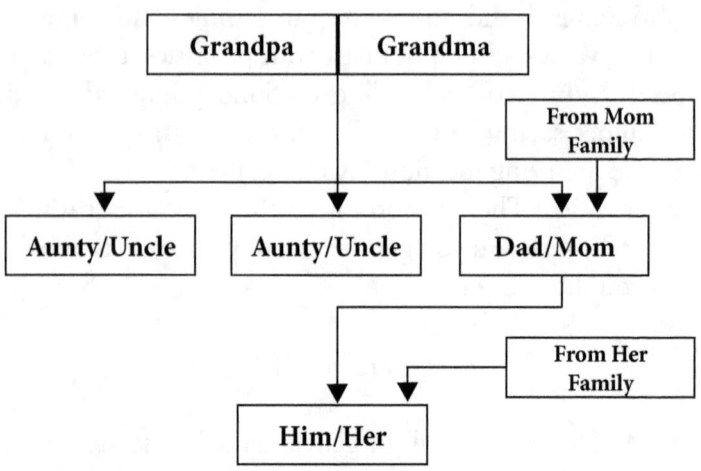

Story: A friend was telling us about how he grew up in an alcoholic home where violence and verbal abuse were the norms. He vowed he would never live that way. Fast forward past the romantic dating, to the spectacular wedding day. Picture the scene, it begins with a toast and continues as the groom continues drinking. By the time the 'loving' couple leaves the celebration, he had become belligerent, aggressive, and horribly drunk. After an unnecessary argument he lands up in handcuffs, and a night of celebrating turned into a night of incarceration. He awoke the next day, sick, both from the heavy consumption and from the realization of who he was becoming, a carbon copy of his dad. He needed to change. The good news is since then with a lot of hard work this couple have altered their legacy through faith in Jesus.

Let me add, I married my mother. Now before you panic, call Adult Protective Services and misquote me, what I mean is I chose a strong, powerful, and beautiful woman. One who is motivational, one who is passionate about her kids and their success. One who loves to dance, has a wonderful sense of humor, one who is fun to be around. One who will protect and defend her family with her life, and also has dark hair!

There is a strong likelihood, if you are a man, you are about to marry your mother and you are heading towards becoming like your father. If you are a woman, you are about to marry your father and you are on the way towards becoming your mother. You will look for qualities in a partner that remind you of your positive past. What you found comfortable, what you enjoyed, what made you feel safe and loved. If your parents gave you that, then it is likely you will seek to replicate it in your marriage partner. That last piece should come with a warning!

> **You marry your mother and become your father, or you marry your father and become like your mother.**

Action: This would be a good time for a transparent and engaging conversation about what really comes down from the previous generations to you. What are some of the values and victories from great, great, great Grandma or what are some of the struggles and stories from great, great, great Grandpa? Go back as far as you can in your genetic line and trace all the good, bad and the ugly. Ask the oldest people in your family for information about who married whom, who died and when. Trace things like cancer, stillbirths, multiple births, divorce, tragedy, faith, success, leadership, etc. You might have some other unique items to map out. Draw it on a schematic of your family tree. Bring them together and examine the canvas on which you begin to draw your unique story as a couple.

Take a look at what Moses, one of the Old Testament greats in the Bible, captured for us from God in Exodus 2 verse 4 to 6:

> *"You shall not make for yourself an image in the form of anything in heaven above or on the earth beneath or in the waters below. You shall not bow down to them or worship them; for I, the Lord your God, am a jealous God, punishing the children for the sin of the parents to the **third and fourth generation** of those who hate me, but showing love to **a thousand generations** of those who love me and keep my commandments."*

He repeats the same sentiment in Exodus 34 verse 7. Notice there is intergenerational movement and affect. A simple example, if a child sees a parent mistreat their spouse, their default behavior will be to treat their spouse in the same way. They will view this behavior as 'normal.' This can take a more profound and more devastating turn when it comes to things like divorce and abuse, just to mention a few.

On the bright side, you will also inherit positive values, like when a family considers Church or faith important. Take note of Pastors or leaders that are third or fourth generation influences. Andy Stanley[2] comes to mind. Notice the impact and power with which they live their lives.

> **You have an affect through the generations, good and/or bad.**

Rod's Story: I remember the season my dad, brother and myself all played on the same field hockey sports team called the Crusaders. It was a blast, I cannot remember the score, but I remember the feeling.

Just recently I had a neat opportunity to play a soccer game with all my children (to be truthful, one of them did a little more supporting than soccer). Unfortunately the soccer side of the family, lost one to the dance side of the family, but we are working at getting her back. This reminded me of my family hockey game, now a generation later.

We must note that some of the influences, or blueprints, passed down can cause an exacerbated challenge for particular couples. Dynamics like cultural group, blended families, socioeconomic class, the role of family, role of husband/father or wife/mother and faith traditions will have a marked effect on the oxygen present in this new family's atmosphere.

The good news is we have seen very successful and happy marriages with all of these dynamics. We know couples who excelled beyond expectations achieving fantastic results within the hardest challenges. These are the inspiring conclusions.

If you are heading into a lifetime together and some of these assumptions and traditions are not discussed, it can lead to negative consequences in the future.

Movement from Self towards Others

Transitioning from a single person world to a marriage culture can be such a shock and adding other pressures from family heritage and lifestyle has the potential to be a show stopper. When you are single, all you think about is yourself. You are consumed with *your* thoughts, feelings, and desires. The moment a person decides to head towards the 'foreign culture' of married life, they have to learn a whole new language and set of norms and values.

> When you are single, all you think about is yourself.

Cheryl's Story: The first small group we ran was

our first spiritual family and our first time living purposefully towards others. We hand-picked some stellar facilitators from my brother Robert's friends, to help us run our first youth group. They were young, cool, fun, and had excellent people skills. We had jobs and a car, two things they didn't, and we all had time, perfect team!

Our weeks consisted of a Wednesday night youth group planning meeting with dinner, discussions, and discipleship. Friday, youth group, that included a debrief with coffee, always topped with leftover ice-cream from the program. Sunday was Church with more engagement. We honestly had no research-based training, we just loved hanging out, sharing ideas, sharing laughs and creating time and space for each other to unpack faith. These relationships gave us the authority to speak into each other's lives. It was never a task, it was never a program, it was life lived out in community. We loved each other as family. These were days that stirred vision that took us on mission around the world. We were a ragamuffin team, but God in His faithfulness used this squad to change lives. Legacy was changed and life trajectories altered. We learned what it looked like to live outwards.

First off, we no longer live for ourselves but for another person. What does that look like in a culture that values women differently from men or men differently from women? What does it look like when there is an 'ex' affecting Holy days and holidays? What happens when one's past spirituality clashes with future religious experiences?

This is all fun and cute in the dating phase when we were 'walking on sunshine,'

> **When you decide to get married you decide to live for another person. You are no longer single.**

possibly even as you read this book. Remember we are actually on our very best behavior and to be honest the best we will behave until a ton of maturing and forming happens. You will not believe us until about 6 months to a year into your adventure. The concrete connectedness of your relationship, after you have said your vows, makes these issues well worth talking through.

Different cultures can have diverse understandings of marriage. This has to be dealt with proactively, or a devastating result is sure to happen. In Africa, for example, there is a cultural group that believes it is entirely acceptable to have a girlfriend when you are married. So the men will have girlfriends in different towns they travel to, with their wives knowledge, because he will have needs that cannot be met by just her. There are also some cultures where the man is the 'all' authority, and she is there to serve him. They live that way. There are others where men have nothing to do with raising the children and others where women are not allowed to work outside the home. Joining together two diverse cultures like this, adds to the adventure, but also the challenge.

Blended families have their own challenges and opportunities. There are many good books written on blended families, and I would recommend you dive into them to understand what is to be expected. An excellent resource is material written by Ron L Deal. Blended marriages involve the merging together of at least four (sometimes more) entirely separate ecosystems that have not had to interact before. The ecosystems of his, hers and his ex and her ex. These are all self-actualized, independent thinking, emotional and at times scared and confused individuals. These invested parties are all be-

> Blended families have their own challenges and opportunities.

ing brought/forced together. They will not all embrace the struggle, they will not all contribute or complement these new decisions and this new direction. You have to be patient, loving, caring and actively listening to your lovely spouse. You need to help each other work through some of the pains and hurts from the past. Become a detective of you spouses battles, scars, and struggles, because you are their mirror and, through God, their healer.

Reaction Styles

Detectives discover! Reaction styles affecting outcomes of all conversations. Tendencies or retorts based on an individuals life stories and experiences. Auto-responses will affect how people engage in conversation. Frustrations can result for a young couple trying to navigate through these exciting waters of becoming one. The conversation might begin well each time but become derailed because of the reply that he or she might emit, and be totally unaware of. Reactions or responses are much like water to a fish. Their reality, the very water they breathe, the very way they do life.

Bad news. Getting anyone to step outside this constructed reality and understand their own reaction is like asking them to climb beyond themselves. Something very tough to do and impossible in isolation.

Good news. This is precisely what God uses marriage for. The unbreakable, no negotiable, sacrificial, loving, intimate, personal, one on one, man and woman life-

> God created marriage, unbreakable, no negotiable, sacrificial, loving, intimate, personal, one on one, man and women lifelong union, for loving illumination for each other.

long union. This space is used by God for loving illumination of each other. Our personal past stories, past pains, past parenting, past relationships, and past perceptions become the 'water' or oxygen we breath. Our reality. This is where there can be healthy reflection and secure safe conversation. God is at work in everybody's story, and our marriages are a big part of that. God has a great and glorious story that He is scripting. We play lead roles. We discover God's characteristics as we discover ourselves through outside eyes.

Within the context of our relationships, we discover how we process relating. This helps us see how we view *God*, and how we are part of His plan. We are God's vessels in the world. He empowers and uses us to facilitate life change. We are here for more than to just live the dream and die. We are here as part of God's fingerprints in the world. The place of greatest person effect is the shaping and molding in a healthy marriage. We get to engage in another humans life to cause reflection and encourage change.

We then get to reflect God to others, firstly in our family and then beyond. Here we embrace our brokenness and engage in self-discovery as God uses us in others lives. We are able to seek out God's vision and solutions as He builds our strength through life's struggles. Here we respond from a place of wisdom, knowledge, and strength with a 'heart after God's own heart.[1]' Here we begin at God, by worshipping 'the Lord your God with all your heart and with all your soul and with all your mind and with all your strength.[2]', and flow His vision outward to 'Love your neighbor as yourself.[3]'

> You are here as part of God's missional solution to your spouse, family and the world. You are His fingerprints.

Traditions

Your closest neighbor is your family. You do indeed marry the 'tree.' Family gatherings create interesting dynamics and come with existing traditions. What about family traditions? What are some of the things that you want to emulate from your birth or adopted family? Are you going to have a real or fake Christmas tree? Are you going to open presents on Christmas Eve? Do you read the nativity story together on Christmas Day? Do you spend the day serving in a soup kitchen? Do you take presents to a local children's hospital? Do you buy each other experiences or 'expensives'? Do you all wear an ugly Christmas sweater? These are just some of the thoughts of only one celebration. We have not even spoken about Thanksgiving, Easter, Memorial weekend, Labor Day, birthdays, Martin Luther King Day, Good Friday, and the national day of left-handed people.

> There are traditions and values you will adopt, there will be new ones you create and there will be some you drop.

Then what about new traditions that you want to form in your new nuclear family? What about an annual global mission trip, family game nights, monthly dinner dates with friends? What happens when your new traditions clash with old family traditions?

Story: One of our traditions is to have a minivan. We have always believed it will be used to invite people to Church or Christian activities. In our attempts to be frugal we would typically purchase a very used set of wheels. Sometimes we were even given a 'soccer' vehicle by concerned citizens who noticed what we were transporting our family and others in. Some would call a ride, one step above a rickshaw.

This one was a classic, not in a 'this is worth something' classic. Just classic in the old, worn down sense. She was a beauty. There was only one major challenge, at random times the sliding back doors would fly open. This would cause the air to rush in and kids to scream. Imagine a combination of a dog with its head out the window and a fighter pilot that opened the cockpit window. There was flapping cheeks, yes, and screams and all round pandemonium. The kids remember me yelling over the noise of rushing air to quit flapping and keep their hands in, are you buckled, hang on tight. I would then hit the brakes, causing the doors to slide back and bang shut. Saved until the next adventure with just a little whiplash residue. I hope this does not become a tradition!

Eloping?

Even if the values and relationships of those close to you are incompatible and challenging to your own, please do not think of eloping. Marrying privately and without fuss might seem to make things simpler but in the long run, the hurts and disconnect could be dragged into the next generation or even many generations into the future. One can have a simple and frugal wedding with a close intimate group without having to rip that experience away from loving family and friends.

As a dad with three beautiful girls, I would be devastated to not be a part of such a precious and Divine moment. There is also a spiritual dynamic that cannot be

> **Family bonds can be affected for many years, even a lifetime with quick or rash decisions.**

overstated. This is greater than family politics and pressures. Not only is there a moment when a beautiful young lady is given away by her father, when she moves from within her Dad's protection and guidance to this new circle of care, but there is also the community that welcomes and affirms this new union. Welcoming them now into their hearts in a new form, a new way. This caring group that surrounds them also holds the man and woman accountable for the pledges they make and calls them up to honor the covenant before God.

> There is something so very powerful about biological community. There is something even more powerful about the multi-generational family. It is a gift!

Elvis in Vegas just does not do justice to this divine institution. Incidentally, Las Vegas is sadly the wedding capital of the world and these marriages are recognized in every country. More than a hundred thousand couples tie the knot in "Sin City" every year. And it is incredibly easy. It takes about 10 minutes to get a marriage license.

Whether you embrace it now or not, it does take a village to raise a child. You cannot do it alone and were not designed to live outside of a community. That is another reason we do not want to break community with family. There is something so powerful when multiple generations come together to love on each other.

Story: We feel that grandparents influence is irreplaceable that we have ours living with us. This is not because they had to, but because we wanted them to.

Now we need to mention there are times when Gramps says the odd inappropriate word, or we lose him in the mall, and there are times with Nana wants to go shopping when we want to rest. But the outcomes and influences on our children have been priceless. The love and devotion that they have for their grandchildren are terrific, and there is nothing like watching Grandma sitting peacefully with our youngest and showing her the classic art of crocheting or knitting. Or Gramps walking them through the finer art of sculpting a colorful garden masterpiece.

Modern Family

This modern world also places some unique pressures on families and marriages with all *too much* possibility for learning and traveling. Vacation days and studies are now never ending because there is always more. Work no longer is done in an apprentice-style where a relationship is solidified and fostered, but now at some remote school of choice. Young people come back full of knowledge and maybe a touch of wisdom ready to take on the world. They find the love of their lives, marry and then get shipped to Germany or Texas with the company. The natural ecosystem is broken.

The global family is new and something of this and future generations. I believe that the adverse effects of this new structure are only just now being observed and measured. More and more people are moving back home towards their original homestead. They have tasted real family and community, and it is too good.

We had no choice. God sent us as missionaries across the world. We had no other option but to respond to His nudge. We dove into a Christian Church community and a small group. It is the next best thing, wherever you are in the world. In a

> **Christian Church community small group is the next best thing to the biological family.**

healthy small group, we found some adopted grandmas, sisters, parents and peers. They are still human and can do silly or even hurtful things, but the good far outweighs the bad. Just give them as much grace as you need from them.

Rod's Story: One time I received more grace than I deserved. I have always wanted to be able to sing. To be honest, my talent lacks far behind my enthusiasm. This one vacation we decided to camp in the green rolling hills of West Virginia. The camping was idyllic with everything including campfires and red sunsets. Sunday came and we decided to find a church to visit and we came across a South Baptist mountain church. It was evident that we were the guests when suddenly twenty 'campers' descended like an army on the front few rows of surprised locals.

The preacher preached his heart out. He then said it was time to sing and invited all who wanted to join the ad hoc choir. I felt like family, I felt accepted, I jumped right up, this was my moment, he wanted me! And he wanted me to *sing*! My girls grabbed my arm and tried to pull me back. Years of dreams and some physical momentum launched me from their grip onto the small stage now full of volunteers and regular Pavarottis. My children slipped further and further down into the pew as I belted out the classical hymns.

The joyful noise was only trumped by the choir shuffle and moves. Think Sister Act meets Pitch Perfect. Might I add that it was well received by my temporary family. I sang my guts out and increased in volume and confidence through the service! I think it's time to cut an album.

Divorce

Divorce is not a good option, and I sincerely doubt whether anyone goes into a marriage, contemplating divorce. The Word of God says that divorce is allowed in two cases [3].

One, where there is infidelity. When one or both have broken the intimate covenant and slept with someone else. This has broken the very oneness that happens through the marriage covenant. Two become one when they have sexual relations. The violation of that unity will cause irreparable damage and pain.

> Divorce is not a good option and I sincerely doubt whether anyone goes into marriage, contemplating divorce.

Action: A great visual and something each couple should just do as an exercise is stick two pieces of Duct Tape together then try to rip them apart. Take note of the result. (Use the real stuff not the cheap tape.)

Two, If the person that you marrying is not a Christian [4]. There is a reliable and powerful warning from the missionary Paul in 2 Corinthians 6 verse 14 :

> *"Do not be yoked together with unbelievers. For what do righteousness and wickedness have in common? Or what fellowship can light have with darkness?"*

These are two extreme cases. The very discussion of divorce should not be taken lightly. Whatever the problems, whatever the challenges that someone faces, divorce, will multiply everything tenfold. Psychologist Diane Medved, in her book The Case Against Divorce, describes the emotional effects of the divorce experi-

> Whatever the problems, whatever the challenges that one faces, divorce, will multiply them ten-fold.

ence:

> "At first you might feel relief," she says, "but it is short-lived. Tests show that for the first five to six years you will be consumed by moderate to severe anger. Depression, which at its very core is a feeling of failure, will be your companion. Stress tests rank separation and divorce as the second and third most traumatic events in a person's life. The only thing ranked more stressful is the death of a spouse."

I cannot stress more clearly and implore more passionately for you to reconsider allowing divorce even to be something that is considered. Do not get me wrong, there will be many difficult times in the future that you will wonder what you were thinking on your wedding day. There will be many times when you cry yourself to sleep wondering if this is what it is, and questioning your sanity.

Documented studies indicate that at least:
- Firstly, in a divorce, your wealth *will half.*
- Secondly, you are going to subject yourself to less free time - *not more* as you cart and carry and coordinate kids and schedules.
- Thirdly, you will spend *more time,* not less time, talking to the one you want to get distance from. You will need to arrange kids, cars, cash and other areas of commonality. Obviously, there are some easier aspects if there are no children or combined assets, but one still has to live with oneself. Plain and simple you have broken the plan, shattered the glass, and unfortunately you will spend the rest of your life putting small dangerous

pieces of shard back together. And as a wise elder once said to me, 'you are wherever you go.'

Rod's Story: As I mentioned before, I am a trained firefighter.

One night, during my training, we decided to go to a dinner and a movie with our close friends Aaron and April Burrell. Cheryl had to quickly rush down town to grab something from her friend Vicky. While there, I heard the fire department tones go off. This meant there was a fire somewhere in the area. Sounding very official, I announced this hot information, of the apparent city combustion.

Strangely enough I thought I began to smell smoke. Remember I had not quite completed my training. I noticed the sirens seemed to be getting closer. I continued to update our party of four that there was really a fire and it was somewhere in the down town. It was only when a large fire truck rushed up with full lights and sirens directly in front of us and the firefighters rushed right past us, right into the building I was standing in front of, that I realized where the fire was. Yes, I was standing at the front door of the three story five alarm fully active fire and did not notice. In my defense it was the back of the building not the front, but still it was a complete loss. Sometimes it can be right behind you or right in front of you and you might miss it. Sometimes you need a mirror, or a wife or some friends to tell you when you are missing the obvious!

This is one reason why living together and marriage are not the same thing. You act and behave differently when the other person is standing with their hand on the exit door. If anything gets too hard, too personal, too painful, they will just use the eject/reject button.

Marriage is designed to be a safe place of commitment and community where you can discover yourself and someone else in the most intimate and personal way. They will know you. They will say and do to you, and with you, things that no other person in the world is given the privilege to do. Your self-consumption, left unchecked will result in your self-justified isolation from humanity because you cannot trust or know the truth about yourself. To quote my friend "Just go live with your selfish self [5]" or from a movie "you cannot handle the truth. [6]"

> You act and behave differently when the other person is standing with their hand on the exit door. If anything gets too hard, too personal, too painful, they will just use the eject/reject button.

Conversely, you could become a person of connection and community. You will have worked out some of your edges. Children, and grand children will enjoy being around you.

Sadly I have been to funerals where people have taken the easy way out, and in their oblivion destroyed every relationship. As the officiant, I doubled the number of guests in the room.

Great News! You are Going to Die

Finally, talk about your death and funeral with each other. We know this does not seem appropriate. We are planning a wedding here! But there are essential things that should be discussed. Do not place that kind of pressure on the one you love, if some unfortunate incident changes the dream. I am not trying to be morbid, and we pray nobody will have to place a spouse in the ground before they are old, wrinkled and seasoned. But the reality is it can and does happen. So let's be ready.

> **Fact: You are going to die someday. I know it is not fun to talk about but let's have a conversation anyway.**

I have a file on my desktop and a copy on my Google docs called 'The End.' I took this idea from my Dad[7]. In it, I placed all important contacts, insurance information and our will and testament. We will talk more about these in the chapter on *Cash*. I also placed a short letter to my children and wife. I update these every now and then. Most of all I want them to know I love them very much and I will see them again one day because of my faith in the Resurrection of Jesus and what He taught us. I also want my funeral to be a celebration. I know where I will be and although it might sound strange, I will not want to be here. I will be in God's presence, so please do not call me back! The apostle Paul states it like this in his letter in Philippians 1:21:

'For to me, to live is Christ and to die is gain.'

End well, so that you can genuinely say, 'till death us do part!'

Speed Notes on Chapter 7

- When you marry your bride, you marry the family. When she says 'I do,' the in-laws do too! There is no way around this, sorry. A conversation about **Clan.**
- It is strange, but as a man you will discover that you marry your mother and you become like your father. And the opposite if you a woman. I hope this is good news.
- You will have a tremendous effect throughout the generations, blessings and curses. Decide what you want to carry onto the next generation, you can alter your genetic line forever.
- You move from singleness and self-actualization to living outwards towards another person. Your life is lived for the other.
- Blended families bring unique dynamics into the new marriage. Explore these and discover the unique needs and blessings.
- Consider the traditions that you bring consciously and unconsciously into the new marriage. Also, decide on some new traditions that you want to create or develop.
- The family and intergenerational community should not be undervalued. We have lost the importance of biological and adopted family in Western culture. This is an untapped resource of wisdom and love. Steal Grandpa out the senior center and wrap him in the family.
- Divorce is not the solution but the beginning of the struggle. Consider carefully this,

as an option. The Bible only gives two cases for exploring this, and they are just for extreme reasons.
- Marriage is a safe place to expose your complete self. You get to see yourself reflected back to you through the eyes of your committed spouse. She or he will not leave when things get tough, and they will!

Action Steps

- Meet with some of the older members of your genetic line and build a family tree looking for highlights and lowlights from the generations.
- Make a list of some of your family traditions. Talk about the values and joys of them. Discuss what ones you want to keep and what ones you want to drop. Come up with some new ones that are unique to you two.
- Have a sensitive 'date' about death. I know, not a fan, that's ok. There are many 'advanced directive' examples online[8]. Fill one out with the dream of only using it when you are old and gray, it might need some revisiting every few years.
- Exercise the spiritual discipline of *Submission*.

CHAPTER 8

Career/Children

You will probably make less of an impact on the corporate world than you dream, but you will male a greater impact on your family than you realize.

Chapter 8

Career/Children

A Conversation about the Rat Race and Rugrats!

Children are wonderful! Their sticky fingers, their ruffled hair, their inappropriate comments, their strange smells, their bumps and bruises, their late night screams, their cuddling and taking all your blankets. Children are part of our eighth conversation and are lovely, especially when they belong to someone else.

> **Children are wonderful and teach us how to live our lives outwards towards others.**

No, children of your own are lovely, and we would not give up our girls for anything. They bring meaning and joy, they bring laughter and new perspectives, they open up new ideas and creative thoughts. They keep us young, they challenge our selfishness, they love on us, they hug us just when we need it, and they are fun to read stories to or watch on the soccer field. They teach us how to live our life outwards towards someone else.

Our love for them is so deep we feel everything. Everything. A beautiful hair day or a broken bone, a delightful date or just a dropped ice cream, we feel it. I once heard it equated with you breaking off a tooth with the nerve exposed. Hot makes it react, cold makes it react, everything makes it react, and the pain shoots through your whole body. That is what life is like having a child. Your nerve is hanging out in space and whatever happens to your child affects you. They are an appendage that goes where it pleases but touches your soul at the same time. I am not sure I can aptly describe what it means to love another human that is independent yet connected, that is alive and from you, yet separate. A beautiful mosaic of yourself and your spouse, yet Divinely conceived and created. I cannot capture in words the feeling of watching this little nugget grow wings and attend college. I cannot describe the emotions of pride, sadness, fear, love and breathlessness one feels when watching your children navigate through life. There are times I just stand at their bedroom door and watch them sleep and thank God for the absolute gift that the biological family is with the additions of procreation. They breathe in and out and they look so peaceful, so content, so amazing. Children are a gift. Life without children, we believe, would lose an enormous amount of beautiful and bright colors. Enjoy them.

Rod's Story: I delivered our firstborn. Well, Cheryl had something to do with it, but being trained as a Paramedic in the army, one of our rotations was with midwifery. So we learned all the essential facts about assisting in a child's birth. Cheryl was fully dilated, and the doctor was standing alongside when I requested the opportunity to deliver her. The doctor delivered her head, cause I did not want to mess that up. I then delivered her shoulders, rotated her torso and brought the rest of her into this world. She was breathtaking. I wept. The incredible beauty, the perfect body, the gusto lungs, the wiggly fingers and toes. I held her, Then I had to give her to mom, she had put in some effort. I then cut the cord and sat down exhausted from all the hard work. I had half a mind to yell out, "Nurse, dab the forehead will you!" Cheryl has no idea how much work delivering a baby is!

There are many times we take them for granted,

there are many times we rush past their unique worlds and fly into ours. Times, like now, we pause, reflect and sometimes regret. There are so many moments we miss and so many opportunities we blow to be present and connecting parents. Children need present parents.

> Children need parents. That means quality and quantity time.

That means quality time and quantity time, just like your marriage. They need the opportunity to think and reflect. They need present parents, sometimes to answer, sometimes listen and sometimes just to be.

The Bible says children are a blessing. Psalm 127 verse 4 and 5 gives us a great visual:

> "Like arrows in the hands of a warrior are children born in one's youth. Blessed is the man whose quiver is full of them."

Not sure how many arrows can fit into a quiver today? Actually, it appears that a quiver would hold three to eight arrows, so a full quiver would be eight. This is starting to feel uncomfortable, right?

When is it time

Only have children when you are ready. Getting the order muddled up causes so much pressure that often the relationship cannot handle it. So in other words, no sex until you are married, and indeed no babies until there are a couple of rings on the 'right' left finger. There are many reasons why this is very important, and we will talk about some of them in Chapter 10 on sex.

Abstaining means the announcement of your pregnancy will be exciting news, not a problem to solve or a dilemma to announce. "I made a mistake Dad, please do not kill George or me, but I am pregnant." Tears, tough decisions, disbelief, questions, and fear are replaced with adventure, excitement, wonder, a big gender reveal, anticipation, preparation, teamwork and beautiful bulging bellies. Some dads have sympathy pregnancies, okay!

> Have babies when you're married and you will enjoy all the dynamics of that. Babies out of order can cause a lot of pain.

Having a baby solo can be done, but ask any single mother or father, and they will tell you how hard it is. The juggling, the loneliness, the late nights and full work days, the fear and the struggle. No baby comes with an owner's manual (except the Bible, and nowhere are there tips on how to change a diaper of an active one-year-old). Each is unique, and each is designed to have a Mom and Dad's care and input. Please have some extra grace and love for those that are forced to do this because of some unforeseen circumstance. But if you have a choice, wait! That's real pro-choice!

What if you cannot conceive?

Some people, no matter how hard they try, cannot have biological children. I have no simple, trite theological answers for you. It is painful and devastating and can be the wreck and ruin of some marriages. I would encourage you to speak to a counselor and be open to adopting or fostering. Many children around the world would do anything to be brought up in your home as one of your clan. Some Churches will help, and there are Christian organizations that will give you some answers.

Abortion, is it an option?

Ironically, while there are so many couples desiring children, around 1 million abortions take place annually in the US alone.

Do not abort! Never! Ever! Why? A few reasons:

> **Do not abort a child! Never! Ever!**

- One: Give it to me! We really would love a little boy. Do not get us wrong, I love our girls, but every Dad wants that son. So give him to us, we would take him in a heartbeat, and there are many others just like us.
- Two: You will regret it for the rest of your life. You will never ever forget. We can only tell you from our experiences of talking to those who made that sad and difficult decision, the pain remains for a lifetime. What is promised as a quick solution to solve a problem becomes a quick way to a lifetime of problems. Everything from depression to substance abuse has been attributed to that one bad decision.
- Three: The child does not belong to you. Theologically we are just stewards of God little creatures. We only get the joy and the privilege to steward God's micro-flock in our homes for a few years, and then they launch off. Killing something that does not belong to you will come at a very high price.

CAREER/CHILDREN

What if I made a huge mistake?

If you have already had an abortion, God has brought you before this text to heal you today. Today we no longer allow the pain of the past to control you. God is the ultimate healer. He understands. God drew your little baby to His heart when it happened. So now it is time to forgive *yourself.* To move forward and to walk in grace and redemption. This means that although you will never ever forget, we are asking God to take the guilt and condemnation away. He is loving and gracious beyond your imagination.

God has enough grace for our mistakes!

The Bible says "For God did not send his Son into the world to condemn the world, but to save the world through him." (John 3:17)

Immediately make an appointment with a Christian counselor and your Church Pastor. You must have some help and companionship as you navigate these problematic memories and thoughts. God has enough grace, but you might not. Make this purposeful and be proactive.

When to have babies?

Our perspective is, wait! We suggest taking a year or two after you get married to discover each other, travel and save. This is a good time to knock a few things off your bucket list and to enjoy this human who has just said yes to you for life. Discover them, love them, connect and cavort. Take that mission adventure, go to Africa, eat strange things, take some risks, enjoy other cultures, go for a care-

Wait to have babies.

free swim at midnight, see a sunrise because you want to and see a sunset because you can. Touch the ocean and kiss in Paris. Return ready to have a fantastic family.

But do not wait too long. We waited longer than we should have. There is a growing group of young couples that slide into a combined narcissism and isolation. They fear the current world and the prospects for their potential kids. They reflect on the pains of their childhoods, and they make a decision not to have children. This is a sad and devastating decision that I believe will haunt them in their silver years. Children are God's way of showing you what it is like to create someone and watch them love you unconditionally. Through your child, you get a small window into a piece of God's perspective and His loving existence.

How many babies to have?

Have babies, and have more babies than you think you want, and if you're asking us, have them closer together. We regret having our girls so far apart. Some of it was due to medical issues and miscarriages. But if we had life over again, we would have twice the number of children, and we would have them close together. And yes, you will never feel ready to bring new life into this world, but go for it, it is worth it! Nobody gave us this advice, so we did not know, but we regret it now.

> **Have babies, and have more babies than you think you want.**

It will be tough, crazy, demanding and exhausting in the first and early years, but each year will get easier and easier. It would be ideal to have one person at home during those first 10 years, however, is not always possible. Family and friends can step up and fill the gap. Remember the African woman and how it takes a village to raise a child? This is time for the village to make a difference.

Rod's Story: That reminds us of the time we visited Port Elizabeth and went out to Aunt Jan's and Uncle Chris's farm. We had a magnificent time enjoying the African wilderness. Enjoyed a hunting, stalk and shoot, adventure and some fantastic farm cuisine. The kids had a blast exploring the surrounding terrain. There were many things to enjoy and discover. We soon had to, unfortunately, board a flight back to the USA and came through the regular border post regiment. Basically, if you declare that you have no meat or dairy products, you are fine. If you have some such products on you, you could be strip searched or worse! We are talking a grave violation. These folks have no sense of humor. This is never something I play around with because we have had too many horrible border post issues, for travelers who try to always follow the rules.

So we head down the green 'nothing to declare' line and past rows of agents, dogs, x-rays, and scanners. A sniffer dog examined our gear briefly as the officer spoke to us. As he ran through the inquisition questions with examining eyes Tamryn tried to interrupt. I told her 'not now' in my stressed parent voice. The rest of the family continued walking and chatting. It was only when we got home and a certain child took out a huge sheep skull and jawbone filled with teeth. This contraband treasure was found on the farm, and revealed with a broad smile. I practically passed out! We brought some deadhead contraband into the country, and I had told the agents we were clean. I felt like I should turn myself in, but I also saw the movie Alcatraz and decided against it.

We would have them close together because, as a family, we would have moved out of the age milestones at the same time, so we would not be dragging a car seat around 20 years after our first. Also, there is a built-in camaraderie and we have found some extraordinary relationships develop in a healthy home with a quiver full of children.

> We would have them close together. We would have them younger if possible.

Later in life, you will not regret those fun-filled family reunions that bring a cacophony of noise and activity with the slews of grandkids and then great and great-great grandkids.

Enjoyment of the generations and the appreciation of the genetic line will only happen if you do not wait until you are 40 to start. Again, if we had a re-run, we would get married young, finish school and college, as a team, sneak in some travel and adventures and then begin having children round about 25. Once you have two or three, they self-entertain, they help each other with dressing and other chores, and have built-in friends and later they can watch each other when you have to run out. Not to Cancun, but at least to get milk.

We have seldom seen an 'only child' who does *not* struggle with acting and feeling like they are God. They have had two adults doting on them, fulfilling their every need, for all their formative years. The result is they believe that they are the most important person in the world, even God! Now, in their minds, they should continue to receive that worship from others in the future. Think about the poor wife for that expectant man or the poor husband for that perceived royalty.

> An 'only child' struggles with a god complex, but many children learn what living in community looks like.

The community of kids also teaches sharing and community above self. They will enter into marriage in a far more open way than a precocious primadonna.

There are a few reality checks that can cause some challenges, including but not limited to the cost in money and time needed to invest in each one of them. We have found that God provides just the right amount, when we are dealing with his little creations, and trusting Him.

Rod's Story: Picture in your mind. A tanned surfer dude with shoulder-length curly golden hair. Add a motorbike, a piecing and throw in some cool moves. Yip, back in the day, that was me, well maybe I was never cool. We lived across the road from the ocean, ran triathlons and went mountain climbing.

Fast forward to today's selfie. Bleached white from living in the Northern Michigan, no surfing in years, driving a minivan and a small eco car. No hair! Six pack is now a rounding bump. And the only mountains I climb are chores and honey do's lists.

Things change, sometimes more than you will believe, so keep the critical things in focus.

One other thing we wish we did better in our younger years was having an open house and living life with open hands. We want our children to know that we have been blessed with much and with so much we can be a blessing to others. So having an open house and open hands means that we are prepared, at any time, to help someone out and to invite someone over. We have begun this with our back door neighbor, and it has been powerful. Living a life towards others is biblical. We also noticed typically the most potent stories our children shared always involved impacting others. We still laugh or cry when we share them with others. Powerful!

We also decided as a part of living outwards was to adopt a Compassion or World Vision child for every child we have in our home. Anna from India and Norminda from South America have already graduated from the program (they were our first), but now we have Bareck, Nityi, Solanga, and little Sofie. You notice we have four and one is a boy, I am still hoping. This draws our children past what they can see to a global community that needs our attention and love. Living outwards.

> Adopt a global child. Change the world one life at a time.

Career, Education + Kids

We have learned, in our modern world, getting a degree is not the end of the conversation when it comes to education. All of us will need to be lifelong readers and learners. Crunching time to be a student, to build your company, to love your spouse and to run after rug rats has the considerable potential of being too much. Getting into a good rhythm will prove helpful. Life has rhythms. Embracing the season you are in and the limitations of your 24 hours will prove wise. Unfortunately, it seems like all the critical things demand a piece of you all at the same time. You will figure out what is essential versus what makes the most noise. One exception, when your wife says I need doughnuts in the third trimester, just get them for her, stat! Setting up your life rhythms to enhance and contribute to what you want to achieve is powerful.

> Become a lifelong learner.

Rod's Story: Empowering your children to be contributors from the youngest age is vital. As soon as they can walk and carry something include them in the process. My little girl would do anything with her Dad, I only learned this on my third, but it was terrific. Chores, she would join me. We shared some time together, just with her, and together we achieved some projects. As long as it was with Dad, she was in, even taking out the trash.

> Empowering your children to be contributors from the youngest age is key.

There was another time when we decided to buy one of our children a double bunk bed. We carried it in under cover of night and assembled the behemoth virtually through the night, for a great morning surprise. Her response was 'meh' at best when she discovered she was not part of the construction. Indeed not the exuberance I expected. But the little wooden Ikea desk we built together she still talks about. We nearly missed this window. They could watch you sweat and struggle and have no unction to do anything or you could building a work ethic and a relationship and, "O yes," you happen to be taking out the garbage.

This is why the career and children discussion is so important. There are some clear facts when it comes to babies: Mom does most of the heavy lifting, literally. What happens if she is the primary breadwinner? What happens if she is a career woman? What happens if she does not want to put the children into daycare? Is it assumed that she will stay home? What about her career? Planning the career path for each of you is vital. Someone needs to continue building a fiscal plan for the family's future. That will be a lifelong investment, first with formal education and followed with continued learning. This ongoing study and extensive education cannot be overemphasized but is also a challenge when life is busy, and kids are small. It seems like you are trying to do everything at once. That *is* God's plan. *You need others.*

Career parameters

Choosing a career that will take you away from home for days, weeks or months at a time will not be the best for raising a family, unless your family travels too! You might have to make some difficult and life-changing decisions. They say the current generation will travel through multiple careers through their lifetime compared to their grandparents who had one or maybe two. It is liberating to say that you do not have to feel stuck in your current position or career. You have options. I encourage young people to bounce around in the first few years because you are still discarding old perceptions of yourself and discovering new ones. It is ok to change jobs, career and even continents.

Legacy

What kind of legacy do you want to leave? Remember there are very few people who actually make a significant contribution in the corporate world. We look at the Bill Gates, etc. of this world and think that is the norm. Work is there for you to feel some personal sense of achievement and to take home a paycheck to enjoy the blessings of a happy home and family. Your boss will not love you like a happy husband or wife. A boss will not need you like a young child. A boss will not run to you at the door and wrap his or her arms around you like your five-year-old, unless there are way more serious issues! That is part of another book.

> **What kind of legacy do you want to leave?**

I believe when it comes to the children, you will spend time with them whether you like it or not. Either on the right side, information and growth, or on the wrong side with cops and cuffs, you choose.

Bringing up children God's way means that you teach the scriptures and the Christian lifestyle to your children. Deuteronomy 11:19 says:

> *'Fix these words of mine in your hearts and minds; tie them as symbols on your hands and bind them on your foreheads. Teach them to your children, talking about them when you sit at home and when you walk along the road, when you lie down and when you get up. Write them on the doorframes of your houses and on your gates, so that your days and the days of your children may be many in the land'.*

> **You will probably make less of an impact on the corporate world, than you dream, but you will make a greater impact on your family than you realize.**

But for you to teach them, you first have to *know them*. The lack of purposeful parenting will cause hurts and wounds in your children. You will wound your children, mostly inadvertently. This will manifest in many different ways throughout their lives. To mitigate this damage, a plan will help. Choosing some goals, and the way you want them to live will help you focus your ideas for them. All your plans/goals should be written down and placed as current priorities on your calendar. A plan without action steps is just a dream. You will easily tell what is important to you by examining your calendar.

A thought for fathers of sons

Fathers call your sons up to be men. Take every moment to affirm their masculinity and expose them to things that will grow their strength and confidence. Celebrate those 'coming of age' moments. At 13 call them into the masculine community and progressively empower him with more responsibilities. When they are 18 or leaving high school embrace that as another moment to celebrate their new independence. Remind him that he is a warrior prince of the King. When he is 21, as a maturing man gather him with your men's small group and speak into his life. Teach him self control, mentor him in wisdom and show him how to treat women. I know he will always be your son, but treat him like the person next to you at work. And finally, the night before he marries his sweetheart, welcome him into the brotherhood of married men that become responsible for each other. Affirm in him of how proud you are of him and that you know he can do it. Give him a copy of the family crest/motto. (some thoughts here spurred on by the book 'Raising a Modern day Knight' by Richard Lewis). These young men will now have a model and a vision for becoming the kind of fathers and husbands that will continue this strong masculine legacy.

> **Fathers call your sons up into masculinity and affirm in them their capability to be a Godly man.**

Rod's Story: I can remember the day my dad said he was proud of me. I was older. I had done a lot of life not knowing if I was able to really live life with masculine strength. I felt ill-equipped to be a man, husband and father. The day my dad said that things changed! He answered a longing in my heart, a yearning and a question that was, until then, unanswered. I know where I was sitting on the couch, I know what he said and I remember how we both felt. Some moments change everything. For me, this was one. The power of a father's words cannot be understated. I felt like a man that day!

CAREER/CHILDREN

A note for mothers of daughters

Please, mothers, draw out of your daughters the profound beauty and depth that is in the heart of every girl, much different from a boy. Affirm her outer and inner glory and how she is a reflection of God. Remind her how capable and wonderful she is. Encourage her to grow in her strength and independence. Remind her that she is a warrior princess of the King. Show her how to love without lust and live without sexuality that is designed for her one husband. Teach her about her allure gift and what it is meant for. At 13 draw her up to think about greater things that are extremely feminine. She will naturally become a woman, but she will not naturally know that she is fearfully and wonderfully made and *worth it*. Worth the efforts and pursuits of a man. She is worth waiting for. She will need to have this spoken into her life because culture screams another message.

> **Mothers affirm and draw out of your daughters the beauty and depth that is there. Note her outer and inner glory that reflects God. Affirm the strength you see in her. Tell her she is worth it.**

We can learn so much from the Spanish traditions with the Quinceañera which celebrates a girl becoming a woman. The elements and symbols remind her that she has transitioned and she now has more significant influence and expectations. When she is 18 or leaving school take her on a date and affirm your trust in her as she heads out into the culture that is toxic for most young people. Talk to her about being an actualized woman and ready to make her mark on society and the world. Tell her your dreams and share your vision for her life taking into consideration what you have seen in her, as she has grown up in your home. At 21 she becomes a peer. Have peer level expectations of her, even though she is always your baby. Then the night before her wedding, pray for her, encourage her, remind her that she is capable and able to do even more than she can imagine. Tell her that you have seen greatness and glory growing in her for years. Remind her that she is part of a community that loves her but that she is set free to be the contributor, wife, and mother God has called her to be, and what a unique gift motherhood is.

Never too late

It is never too late. Never too late to adopt a child and change a life. Never too late to start a career, remember Colonel Sanders of Kentucky Fried Chicken, he was 65 when he started and so was Laura Ingalls Wilder who wrote Little House on the Prairie.

> **It is never too late!**

It is easier when you are younger and pumped full of energy, vision, and optimism. Choose wisely your career and choose wisely your spouse and then enjoy the adventure with both its ups and downs and there will be many of both. But with God, you will be able to put your hands in the air and yell loud with exhilaration, like you are at a Carnival or Cedar Point. Enjoy!

CAREER/CHILDREN

Speed Notes on Chapter 8

- **Children** are wonderful and necessary to teach us how to live outwards towards others.
- Children need both parents, and they need present parents with quality and quantity time.
- Do not have babies out of order. No sex until the wedding. Having a baby before the wedding will cause all kinds of tension and stress. Babies should bring only joy and jubilation.
- Abortion is not God's plan, and should never be an option. Your baby could be a blessing to someone who is unable to fall pregnant or wants another child.
- Wait for a few years after getting married to have children, so you can discover each other, and enjoy the time as a young couple, not too long, but enough to knock off some bucket list things and to mature.
- Now have babies! Have more than you think you want. A full quiver is really 8, but that would scare me too.
- Empower your kids to be contributors, not consumers or they will struggle for the rest of their lives, and it does not give you time to find life balance.
- Be a continued learner and do not be afraid to change careers.
- Fathers do something that only Fathers (men) can do, and that is, *call masculinity* out from your son.

- Moms call out inner and outer glory from your daughters and affirm their strong femininity.

Action Steps

- Take her on a date, and open up the discussion about career and children. Make a note of the vision God has for you as a team, and develop a plan. Understanding that most times you have to tweak and change it, but have a target. Plan to have your babies in the right way at the right time.
- Visit a homeless shelter for kids in your area, especially those facilities that take kids under 18 that have been rejected out of the foster system for some reason. Try to get to hear some of their history and story.
- Explore a Compassion International or World Vision child.
- Exercise the spiritual discipline of *Worship.*

CHAPTER 9

Cash

God gives us 100% of what we have in time, treasure (cash etc.) and talents. He lets us use His resources to do life. Be wise.

Chapter 9

Cash

A Conversation about Bringing Home the Bacon

Budgets and buying, building and borrowing, and all the other dynamics of handling your cash will challenge your marriage, more than any other topic you discuss in your blissful union. This is the one topic that has the potential to destroy any happy couple. Let us have our ninth conversation about **Cash**.

> **Create a Budget, it will save your marriage.**

Here are 'Ten Commandments' for handling your money. Helpful ideas, to stay married and not end up in money madness.

One
Do not spend more than you make.

Rod's Story: This has been a struggle for us. I am a visionary and Cheryl, an optimist, so we have dabbled in everything from direct sales to pyramid marketing schemes. We always believe that we will crack the code, solve the puzzle, be the one. We will be able to make money where others have not because we are more dedicated, more motivated. We still quote one of the conferences to this day. They had us stand and sing a tag line "I'll take you higher, my friend, than ever before!" over and over again. We were a little suspicious that some were

> **Do not spend more than you make.**

already higher than they should be.

This might sound relatively simple and intuitive, but ironically most of us have around sixteen thousand dollars in credit card debt. (USA today October 2016[1]) In fact, we had closer to 20K before we got serious. Let's make this simple: People do not have money are spending as if they do! They are placing it on credit cards. These infamous credit cards are securing something for them, something they did not expect. It is securing pain, payments, and problems! They cannot use cash because they are buying with money they do not have.

> **People that do not have money are spending as if they do!**

Credit Cards are from satan, be very careful of these. They are designed by actuaries to reel you in, eat you up, spit you out, and steal the shirt off your back while they are about it. Why do you think there are so many 'gifts' when you use their card? They have worked it out, you will pay for it somehow, someday, sometime. They are patient, they will wait for that one tough month, that one emergency decision, that one spontaneous buy, that day after Thanksgiving sale and then you are in too deep, and you will pay! And you will pay again, and again. Do you know it takes the average family about 10 years to pay off $10,000.00 in credit card debt, at a minimum payment plan it will take 12 years?

> **Credit Cards are from satan.**

They justify spending *more* than they are earning because there is an apparent emergency need.

The Bible is evident in this principle. Proverbs 22 verse 4 says

"The rich rule over the poor, and the borrower is slave to the lender."

Have you ever decided *not* to pay up on a debt? You know you will receive a visit from Vinnie that might include broken bones and concrete! How much does that feel like freedom? How much does that feel like the American dream?

So our first goal was to sit together and create a budget. At times a challenge, but this budget had to be decided collectively and in consensus. And has to *zero out*. There is a draft budget template at the end of the chapter by Dave Ramsey[2] and the Crown Financial Money Map[3].

Second
Give God first, yourself second and the rest, the rest.

Give God at least the *first* 10% of your earnings. This is another biblical principle and here are two scriptures to stretch your thinking. Genesis 28 verses 20 to 22:

> **Give God first, yourself second and the rest, the rest.**

> *"Then Jacob made a vow, saying, "If God will be with me and will watch over me on this journey I am taking and will give me food to eat and clothes to wear so that I return safely to my father's household, then the Lord will be my God and his stone that I have set up as a pillar will be God's house, and of all that you give me I will give you a tenth."*

There are many more verses that reflect this sentiment. The New Testament takes it one step further in 2 Corinthians 9 verse 7:

> *"Each of you should give what you have decided in your heart to give, not reluctantly or under compulsion, for God loves a cheerful giver."*

This is where you will find some people increasing their giving, some well beyond 10%. They have received generously and want to be faithful and cheerful about giving it back. I know of people that give away 50% of their income. Pastor Rick Warren from Saddleback Church in California, once said that when he began working, he gave God 10% of what he made and then increased that by 1% every year. This should make you wonder if God really wants you to purchase that extra packet of Doritos.

Rod's Story: Rob, my brother-in-law, actually began giving 10% of his money away even before becoming a Christian because he just saw the result of being faithful. God's principles stand. It has been great to watch him find faith and then continue to give and see how God has blessed him, and his wife, in many ways. So much so that they were the ones who enabled us to purchase our first real house in America. God blessed a faithful heart and family.

We sometimes forget that God gives us 100% of what we have regarding time, treasure (cash, etc.) and talents. He lets us use *His* resources to do life. We decide and enjoy what we are going to do with it, but *none* of it really belongs to us. We are the custodians of God's blessings in our lives, and we have the benefit of using

> The theology is that God gives us 100% of what we have in terms of time, treasure (cash etc.) and talents. He lets us use His resources to do life.

His checkbook (cash) in *our* lives.

We decide the amount, and give God first. Making it *automatic*. It comes right out of our bank account, on the day after payday, or we never will. Why? Because we have the strange habit of moving the boundary fences as our income changes. Note giving also comes with a promise of provision and abundance. Malachi 3:10 :

> "Bring the whole tithe into the storehouse, that there may be food in my house. **Test me in this**," *says the Lord Almighty, "and see if I will not throw open the floodgates of heaven and pour out so much blessing that there will not be room enough to store it."*

We attempt to pay *ourselves* next by allocating 10% to savings. This can take the form of investments and/or a cash savings account. But we make it an account that *cannot* be easily accessed or we would be tempted to dip into it when the first emergency fast food craving hits us, like today. We encourage our children with an early investment start, as it is going to make a big difference in the value of their future finances. Start right away, even if you are reading this with a few years under the belt. When you are 14-18 years of age, investing for house payments is better and wiser than buying the next video game even though it might be hard to visualize when you young. Trust us on this one!

> **Pay yourself next.**

College loans can be kept to a minimum or zero by working hard for scholarships. Completing college classes at school (complete your Associates by 12th grade), working while at school and being frugal and wise will enable you to embrace each life phase more completely. You can also literally move in with Dad. I am not

> **Get rid of school debt, aggressively.**

kidding. The Bible presents a picture of the man, once betrothed, building onto his family's home to accommodate himself, new bride and children. This would enable resources to be shared. Take a look at the investment growth chart at the end of the chapter. Note the exponential curve and how an early start effects it.

Then we *pay the rest with the rest*. So use the remaining 80% of our resources to cover costs for the house, vehicles, food etc. They will always be there, and you will be surprised how we adjust our lifestyle based on 'what is left,' and so should you.

> **Pay the rest with the rest.**

Action: How much more do you need to be financially strong? Just another $10,000, right? We all believe that we just need $10,000 more? But as you are wishing, here is the kicker, someone else is already earning that extra $10,000. And guess what, they are also hoping for just $10,000 more themselves. And someone has $10,000 less than you, wishing they could just earn *just what you do!* Take a moment to ponder your income and blessings. Think about what God has already done for you.

A quick note: depending on what life phase you are in, these percentages (10, 10, 80) could be a little different. For example, if you are young and single, you might be able to give more and save more. If you are more mature, with children, you might have to keep it very tight. But make it *automatic*.

Thirdly
Plan for emergencies, because emergencies happen to everyone.

There is nothing more consistent than the unexpected. Emergencies will come, and when they do, they should not destroy you or a great marriage. It could be a broken washing machine, a house fire, vehicle accident or medical expenses. They will all call for immediate cash input. Most financial speakers suggest an emergency fund of $1,000.00 and then to build it up to *3-6 months of living expenses*. Placing some money into your emergency fund every month will relieve a tremendous amount of stress. Make this *automatic*. We are far from making this a reality but are working towards it. This might be because Cheryl considers a 'vacation need' an emergency!

> **Plan for emergencies because emergencies happen to everyone.**

Fourthly
Take out limited term life insurance.

Protect yourself and your spouse from financial ruin. This is not expensive cover but would be lifesaving in the event of a disaster. If one or both of you happen to die, we would not want to leave those left behind carrying a heavy financial burden, alone, on top of grieving. For less than $100 per month, my wife and I each have a $500,000.00 life policy, which pays out if either of us dies. This is a limited term (15 years) policy. Now I only have to sleep with one eye open. Set this up and make it *automatic*.

> **Take out limited term life insurance.**

Fifth
Use cash only.

This sounds old school, but if you only spend what

you have in your hands you will not be caught with exceeding your financial capabilities. Many of the traditional money and budget plans will encourage some form of

> **Use cash only.**

an 'envelope' system. This is literally placing cash for each of your monthly budgeted expenditures into a physical envelope. When you need grocery money, you take it out of that grocery envelope, until it is finished. The same with gas, recreation, etc. This creates a clear boundary or limit. Sometimes these amounts need to be altered as you do life, but this gives you a starting point. Remember if the budget balances you know there will be no stealing from car repairs to buy cookies. Although, according to my wife, cookies are in fact more important than car repairs, especially if they are chocolate chip.

Sixth
Bigger is not better.

Simplify, simplify, simplify. We swim in a culture of discontentment. We are taught before we can walk that we 'deserve' only the best and loads of it. We are, somehow, owed all our

> **Bigger is not better.**

eyes see. So we gather and get, we collect and clutter. We increase our debt and our depression, fatigue sets in and that soon leads to a feeling of being overwhelmed. Stuff literally sucks the energy out of us[4]. We gather more and more 'necessary junk' until we have filled the garage. Now it can no longer house a vehicle! Stressed we now rent a storage unit to store our garbage. Apparently, we do not really need these items otherwise we would not be pushing them into deep, dust covered, forgotten storage, right?

What would it look like to get a house smaller than

you want? What would it look like to drive used vehicles? What would it feel like to shop at a Goodwill, the Salvation Army or your local gently used clothing store so you can live debt free? Join the trend!

Buy a super small house.

Now instead of spending hours cleaning and moving and searching through all the household 'treasures,' you can invest in some rich relationships.

We have never bought a new car. New vehicles lose so much of their value just taking them off the lot. Here is an idea, buy a cheaper used car first, then pretend you have a car payment just like the one you would have if you bought the car of your dreams. Now place *that* in *your* account until you have enough to pay cash for it.

Buy a used car only.

Seventh
Invest in experiences not 'expenses.'

It is fun to get a new tennis racquet, it is neat to get a flashy watch, but what will be remembered will be the times spent with others. There is more value and reward from a shared adventure than a shared acquisition. Yes, we need to invest in certain things to do life. A family car is essential but what is more exciting is the adventures that car takes you on.

Invest in experiences not 'expenses'.

But we *have* also got to spend some money. It's a must! Do not be too miserly! Life is enjoyable, so use some cash! Make it fun. Once you have done the hard work and been wise, then spend, in your categories, with joy and excitement! Go for it! Cheryl is fantastic at this!

Spend some money!

Rod's Story: I cannot remember many of my dad's vehicles growing up, but I can remember the cruise my parents took us on when I was 10. I can remember so many elements of it. I can still see the layout of the boat, I remember playing shuffleboard on deck. I can see my brother dropping his toy car overboard and it getting smaller and smaller, then sinking. The movie onboard was Airport 77, not the comedy but the one where they get trapped under the ocean. Now, who thought that was a good idea? I can also remember getting lost on the multiple decks with my baby sister, I guess that is relative, as at some point you run out of boat. I can almost savor the good food again. But I cannot tell you what car we drove to the dock in!

Investing in experiences with your spouse, family, and friends will bring so much more joy than upgrading your flatscreen. An adventure shared, brings many times the pleasure!

Eighth
Live generously. Invest in others.

How much can you give away? What would it look like to live in such a frugal way that you can give more of your time, talents and treasures? What would weekends look like if you were not trying to work 80 hours or that second and third job but were able to pour yourself into others? How would you feel if you had the space to look for God moments with yourself and your spouse? Jesus gave His life for you, can you give your life for Him? Look local and global!

> **Live generously. Invest in others.**

Story: We once heard a speaker share the story of a family who was very frugal and saved money. They just kept praying for God to use them and kept putting the money away. Then one day, once they had collected $10,000.00, they happened to be in a conversation with a new young couple at church. The couple mentioned they had been wanting to adopt a baby for some time and everything was looking good except they needed $10,000.00 to complete the process.

The couple knew what they were called to do and why God had them put money away. So they asked if they could come over later that day to the young couple's house. A rather strange and imposing question considering they had just met each other. Once there, they hand-delivered a $10,000.00 check to this new young family so they could adopt a little orphan child into Godly community. Five lives were changed forever and a legacy altered, that day!

Ninth
Retirement planning and saving is not optional.

Investing a small amount every month from your 20's will pay high dividends in the future. Do not be unwise when it comes to this. It sounds romantic to say we will live on love and fresh air. In reality the last season of your life is costly and typically not discussed until it is too late. Make contact with an investment advisor today. We want you to be able to retire financially sound, not for picking up shells on the beach or watching another margarita seasoned sunset, but so you are free to invest your life in others as God leads. Make this *automatic*.

Ten
Live Debt Free.

Debt is from Satan. It enslaves us and makes money our master. Do Not Borrow! Pay Cash. The Bible puts it like this in Proverbs 22:7:

> **Live Debt Free.**

"The rich rule over the poor, and the borrower is slave to the lender."

Rod's Story: We were looking to buy or rent a house. We found one that had a beautiful big barn and even some horses. After checking out the house, we asked about the four-legged friends. The owner said that she boards them and that we are welcome, as part of the deal, to ride them anytime. 'They all needed to be ridden more than they were,' she said. Bonus! No problem, I had ridden horses as a kid so this would be 'like falling off a horse', so the expression goes. Cheryl was far more cautious and counseled against it. I said 'Simmer down Filly, this is going to be awesome!' I got the look!

I led the first horse into the barn and placed a saddle on her. All was proceeding well and going according to plan. In my mind, I was already riding in the Kentucky Derby. I remember thinking not to show the beast my anxiety or fear, right? I noticed my daughter, right next to me. She would surely love to ride, so I placed her onto one of the saddles and walked her horse out into the pasture.

Turns out I miscalculated a few things. Firstly, this filly looked like she wanted to have a saddle and rider on, but, actually she wanted to run free. Secondly, running around loose in the pasture, the other horse, suffered from some great jealousy and came running up to her and bit her on the butt. Thirdly, in my scurry to care for my child on the new bucking bronco, I grabbed her and placed her on the other side of the enclosure. It was only then fourthly, that I noticed as I tried to step through the fence that it was fully electrified! Yelping, jittering and screaming like a kid I escaped the thunderous hooves to lie on the ground in the fetal position while Cheryl stood there laughing her head off.

As you are developing your financial portfolio, track it and document it. A helpful tool I learned from my dad, and mentioned briefly earlier, is to try to capture essential and useful information in a file labeled "THE END." **Develop a legal plan.** You can store this file wherever you wish but make sure your loved ones know about it. Place in it important accounts, insurance policies, title deeds, copies of passwords, identity documents, web access links and anything else you think would be helpful if you were to drop dead tomorrow. Remember the Bible says that you are not guaranteed tomorrow[5]. Pay attention to the security of where you place this. We should not live in fear of death, but being prepared for it will be a great blessing to your loved ones left behind. Putting your final plans in a will is also money well spent.

How fantastic would it be to leave a substantial fiscal legacy and vision for your family? **End Well.**

Unfortunately, the converse would be a busy person, working three jobs to save some money, but in doing so, is not able to spend time, in good health, with loved ones. All the savings in the world would not be worth it.

Speed Notes on Chapter 9

- It sounds crazy, but if you make $10 bucks it does not make sense to spend $11, it's not yours to spend. Have a conversation about **Cash**!
- Honor God by giving Him first, and create a budget that balances to $0. This comes with a biblical blessing[6], each month, *automatically*.
- Life happens, plan for it by packing some money away each month, *automatically*.
- Limited Term Life insurance is not expensive when you're young, but it is costly if you need it and you do *not* have it!
- Using cash is a good discipline to help you remain within budget.
- Buy smaller than you want, less than you want, so you can live as you want! Clutter Kills!
- Experiences have more value than expenses, especially if you're paying them off years later. Have a life of adventures.
- Live outwards, towards others. A generous attitude will help you see God's fingerprints in many everyday moments. Why pay it forward only at Christmas, you can have fun all year!
- Planning for the future is vital. Electing not to plan, by default, is a plan to fail. Getting this wrong will be very costly when you are too old and cannot reboot.
- Debt is from satan! Use a budget and some banking tips and hacks.

Action Steps

- Open some free bank accounts, check in at your local branch for more information.
- Have a date and develop a combined family budget!
- Make as many of your transactions *automatic* as possible.
- Create your 'envelope system', so you do not make automatic silly purchases!
- To use the words of Dave Ramsey, sell everything you can, so much so, that the kids think they are next. Simplify and lighten your life.
- Attend a Dave Ramsey Financial Peace Class after the wedding.
- Exercise the spiritual discipline of *Simplicity*.

Budget Example

This example is with percentages using the 10, 10, 80 Rules (Give 10, Save 10, live on 80)

10-15%	GIVING
5-10%	SAVING
25-35%	HOUSING
5-10%	UTILITIES
5-15%	FOOD
10-15%	TRANSPORTATION
2-7%	CLOTHING & Gifts
5-10%	MEDICAL
5-10%	PERSONAL
5-10%	DEBTS-to retire them

Now complete your monthly budget together.

Him	INCOME	_____
Her	INCOME	_____
TOTAL	INCOME	_____
10-15%	GIVING	_____
5-10%	SAVING	_____
25-35%	HOUSING	_____
5-10%	UTILITIES	_____
5-15%	FOOD	_____
10-15%	TRANSPORTATION	_____
2-7%	CLOTHING & GIFTS	_____
5-10%	MEDICAL	_____
5-10%	PERSONAL	_____
5-10%	DEBTS (to retire them)	_____
TOTAL	EXPENSES	_____

Difference (Income-Expenses - SHOULD = $0.00)

Investment Example Explained

Notice that the 19 year old places in $2,000.00 a year for 8 years and not another dime, an investment of $16,000.00 at 12% compound interest.

The 25 year old waits and places $2,000.00 a year until they were 65 an investment of $78,000.00, an added investment of $62,000.00.

The teenage investor retires with significantly more than the person who waited until 'they could afford to'. Take notice of the incredible difference at 65.

CASH

Investment Example[7]

Age	Invest	12%	Invest	12%
19	$2000	$2240	$0	$0
20	$2000	$4749	$0	$0
21	$2000	$7558	$0	$0
22	$2000	$10706	$0	$0
23	$2000	$14230	$0	$0
24	$2000	$18178	$0	$0
25	$2000	$22599	$0	$0
26	$2000	$27551	$0	$0
27	$0	$30857	$2000	$2240
28	$0	$34560	$2000	$4749
29	$0	$38708	$2000	$7558
30	$0	$43352	$2000	$10706
31	$0	$48554	$2000	$14230
32	$0	$54381	$2000	$18178
33	$0	$60907	$2000	$22599
34	$0	$68216	$2000	$27551
35	$0	$76802	$2000	$33097
36	$0	$85570	$2000	$39309
37	$0	$95383	$2000	$46266
38	$0	$107339	$2000	$54058
39	$0	$120220	$2000	$62785
40	$0	$134646	$2000	$72559
41	$0	$150804	$2000	$83506
42	$0	$168900	$2000	$95767
43	$0	$189168	$2000	$109499
44	$0	$211869	$2000	$124879
45	$0	$237293	$2000	$142104
46	$0	$265768	$2000	$161396
47	$0	$297660	$2000	$183004
48	$0	$333379	$2000	$207204
49	$0	$373385	$2000	$234308
50	$0	$418191	$2000	$264665
51	$0	$468374	$2000	$298665
52	$0	$524579	$2000	$336745
53	$0	$587528	$2000	$379394
54	$0	$658032	$2000	$427161
55	$0	$736995	$2000	$480660
56	$0	$825435	$2000	$540579
57	$0	$924487	$2000	$607688
58	$0	$1035425	$2000	$682851
59	$0	$1159676	$2000	$767033
60	$0	$1298837	$2000	$861317
61	$0	$1454698	$2000	$966915
62	$0	$1629261	$2000	$1085185
63	$0	$1824773	$2000	$1217647
64	$0	$2043746	$2000	$1366005
Totals	**$16 000**	**$2 288 996**	**$78 000**	**$1 532 166**

ELEVEN C'S FOR A STRONG MARRIAGE

CHAPTER 10

Cuddles

*Sex is good, natural and ordained by God.
Thank you God!*

Chapter 10

Cuddles

A Conversation about Sex and Stuff

Someone once said: "Love is an ice cream sundae, with all the marvelous coverings. Sex is the cherry on top."

Sex is that fantastic. What a great job, God! Let's jump into the next conversation about Cuddles.

> **Sex is fantastic and God's idea.**

What a fun way to enjoy each other and bring children into the world. Have you thought about the fact God could have made us procreate with a handshake? A simple "greet each other" on a Sunday morning could result in 20 or more offspring. Or God could have made you self-procreate, like certain jellyfish, sea anemones or flatworms.

No, God placed babies within the context of a union of two loving people. I can only imagine the conversation between the triune Godhead:

Imagination Story: God says, "Jesus and Holy Spirit, I have a great idea for humanity. What if I gave them the ability to enjoy such unity as we enjoy in our Triune Nature? What if it involves three pieces, the man, the woman, and Our Presence? What if when we bring them all together, they form a strong and secure covenanted relationship? What if within this secure circle, this edifying encouraging union, we place a new life? This new life can look like them and reflect them."

Jesus, "Whoa."

God continues, "What if, in this way, they get to

experience, in just a small way, the joy and excitement we enjoy bringing creation into being? And what if the very act of creating this new life will need them to be the closest any human has been to them, face to face, body to body, where they feel each other's heartbeats? What if, in fact, they have to become one and literally enter into one another?"

Holy Spirit responds, "Now that's close!"

God says, "What do you think about that? Wouldn't that be something so enjoyable, so intimate, so powerful and so exhilarating? At that moment they will virtually feel the closeness of our existence!"

God continued, "Hold on, there is more, now look at this. How about, only in this heightened connectedness, can the man then actually release himself, right into her. Only in this safest secure environment can she truly receive him into herself. The moment will be so moving, so invigorating, face to face, body to body, skin to skin. He will actually breathe her breath, she will taste his saliva, and at that moment every muscle, every nerve, and every thought will bring into being a new moment of creation."

Jesus responds, "Momentus!"

God, "And then how about we give woman a chance to carry this brand new creation. Let her feel the growth and life within her. This is such a unique and powerful experience I am sure she will marvel at it every day of her life. Just think, she will birth from within herself the very product of their loving and closeness. She will carry and then release the mosaic creation that belongs to them both. They will feel like creators. It will be in their image like they are in Ours. And just think how the father will feel the first day he can hold this miracle in his hands! He will see his features and see this new life. Wow, I think that will be something that he will never forget."

Holy Spirit shouts, "Just do it!"

We have noticed that unfortunately, God's pure and delightful creation of sexuality has been warped by humankind.

Women are taught, through music, media, and misinformation their bodies and sexuality should be used to gain attention. This attention will give them power. This fake addicting power will remind us of the garden of Eden. They are taught the gift of allurement given to them by God for the use of sexual intimacy with their husband should just be prostituted out in culture. All for improper gains. They have been encouraged and even shamed for not 'sexing it up'. Have you noticed Halloween dress up, dance attire and bathing suits, just to mention a few? Today everything from businesses to local billboards use sexuality and sensuality to sell.

> The world has distorted women's sexuality. Their gift of allurement has been prostituted in culture.

Pornography is another major agent of deforming God's original and pure use and design for sexuality, something I was unfortunately exposed to at an early age.

The Bible is full of references about the role and enjoyment of sex. We found that it is always placed within the context of a committed marriage. It was designed for pleasure and procreation.

Beginning in Genesis we see God speaking about two separate self-actualized humans uniting so intimately He calls them 'one flesh'. This closeness, this unity, reflects the bond of two people but also echoes the unity within the Trinity. This is God's context. The book, Song of Solomon, in the Bible, highlights for us the enjoyment and delight of this wonderfully crafted gift. The language is poetry and the imagery startling, for a Holy book. It reminds us God is not embarrassed or shocked by sexuality, it is His idea!

This author builds a picture of a man's enjoyment

and his woman's absolute beauty. He marvels at her eyes, is captured by her hair. Her smile takes his breath away, and he admires her teeth. The very shape of her head, her beautiful nose, he observes. He ponders every contour of her face. He muses over how sweet and succulent her kiss is, and he notices his enjoyment of her breath. Kissing her is like drinking nectar. There is clearly an appreciation for her physical form. He is enamored by her physical beauty. Her neck is spellbinding, and her breasts cause him excitement. He marvels at them and touches and caresses them. He enjoys the feeling and the look. He speaks of her belly and how he finds it so enjoyable, and her waist so inviting. He then ends with the 'mountain of myrrh and the 'hill of incense.' We will let you unpack that ultimate enjoyment and experience. I am not making this up!

Action: Read Song of Solomon, together, it might just make you blush. God created sex. But He created it within a specific context.

Song of Solomon details not only the elements of lovemaking but some ways to 'do it'. The story is of a woman that is in love with the King. The love conversation goes back and forwards as they discover each other and progress from love to intimacy.

> Read the Old Testament Bible book called Song of Solomon, it gives a grand vision of sex, and it's in the Bible.

Excited Love

She warns however that 'love excited' is only meant for when it can be satisfied. Do not allow "excited love" until you are married. Women excite love by activating their allure gift, and men excite love when they respond to that alluring. Until marriage, a woman is to reserve her sexual allure and a man is not to respond in that vein, lest they stoke up 'love excited' when they are not ready. Protect yourself from releasing the love before it is due. Song of Solomon 3 verse 5b:

> *"Don't excite love, don't stir it up, until the time is ripe—and you're ready."*

> **Do not excite love until you are ready to satisfy it.**

Dating

Rod's Story: We dated horribly! I was continuously and inappropriately on the hunt. I told you about some of the negative and perverted influences in my life. I was always pushing my desires on Cheryl. I was actually trying my utmost to 'excite love'. I was definitely passionate for her. I tried to move the boundaries all the time.

I remember the one time I convinced her to 'park', at a spot a little off the beaten path. We had both come from work, and it was fairly late on a Friday night. We were hanging out, chatting, and listening to music. At a certain time in the evening, when I felt she was hypnotized by my moves and magic, I activated my romance mixed tape (this was before playlists). The vibes were smooth and the atmosphere perfect for my 'attack'. After some kisses and cuddles, we actually fell asleep.

We were awoken to the stern voices of the local police department knocking on the steamed up windows. I thought I was going to be arrested, Cheryl was embarrassed and not impressed. Needless to say, I got an icy shoulder, and we drove home in silence.

One of the most significant issues we have with the modern day version of dating is it seems like men and women are out there trying their best to activate or "excite love" in each other. They do this so they can feel valued, desired and wanted. Some think they need this just to know they exist. This often arises out of a void left by absent parenting or a breakdown in the home. Being loved, being accepted, being respected will never be attained through sex in and of itself. Ironically when sex is used to fill childhood gaps or insecurities, it does not build up but breaks down. This makes the difference between need and realization larger. Sex is beautiful and wholesome in the right context. Never, never shameful or embarrassing within the context of marriage. On top of that, most of the 'on again,' 'off again,' style of romantic dating amongst young people really is a form of practiced divorce.

What follows are some thoughts on sex:

Sex is good and from God

If your experience is any different or has been shaped by abuse, please make counseling a priority. Sex in marriage is to be enjoyed and celebrated. There are negative consequences if sex, as God intended, is distorted.

Sex is about exploring, enjoying and being enjoyed by another person

1 Corinthians 7 verse 5 says:

> *"Do not deprive each other except perhaps by mutual consent and for a time, so that you may devote yourselves to prayer. Then come together again so that Satan will not tempt*

Sex is good and from God. Sexual enjoyment and satisfaction can be distorted by intimacy hurts from your past.

you because of your lack of self-control."

It is not right to deprive each other. Other scriptures caution about your attitude towards your body. Your body now belongs to your spouse, and their body belongs to you. When you are one, you are one! Explore each other. Enjoy every detail and dimple, created for your enjoyment. Check out Song of Solomon again. Take time to discover and delight in what makes him feel good, and what makes her feel loved.

Rod's Story: I have hurt Cheryl with demanding, unkind or insensitive words. This has had a significant impact on her self esteem and image through the years. A thoughtless word or action can cause a lifetime of hurts.

Sex is more than penetration, good sex takes time

Good sex is about touching the heart before touching the 'mountain of myrrh.' As time has progressed I have learned that getting to know, love and understand the love of my life, is the adventure that leads to great sex. Mark Gungor says that if you want great sex, begin the day before. You can have McDonald's but wouldn't you rather have Thanksgiving Dinner! Great sex means investing the time in loving your spouse. It is not about using each other.

> Sex is about touching the heart before touching the 'mountain of myrrh'.

Sex has rules

Rather skip when he or she is tired, hungry or under time pressure. Sex in 5 minutes for 5 minutes is not good.

'Hey, you awake', is not a good start. I did not know this and one time woke the bear!

Sex is about getting naked

All through Song of Solomon, you are hearing about a man and then a woman enjoying each other's lines and curves. It's a celebration of form and shape. God did a great job when He formed and shaped man and woman. There is admiration and intrigue as each explores the other. This is normal and biblical. Be naked! Be very naked! Ladies, he chose you just like you are, so strut your stuff. This can be easier said than done, men be gentle and patient here.

> Sex is about getting naked, so get very naked and enjoy the lines and shapes God created.

Wedding night sex is bad

Yep, I blew this one! Temper your expectations around sex on your wedding night and consider waiting one more night after which you will be fresh and refreshed. Wedding days are exhausting. You are both tired and have been on your feet since the crack of dawn. You have been organizing, smiling, moving, dancing, talking, greeting, sharing and laughing. Consider resting, relaxing and recharging for a radical rendezvous the next night.

Virgin sex or first time sex can be less than anticipated

When a couple is new at being intimate, they have not learned how to love each other well, yet. There is a learning

> There is a learning curve, with sex, that takes some time.

curve, with sex. This takes some time. The first experience is not what it looks like in the movies, ever. She can be nervous because she wants it to be just right. He can be anxious because he wants her admiration and satisfaction. This could lead her to be dry, distracted and 'all in her head', this could lead him to be premature and regretful. It can take some time for both to feel satisfied at about the same time. Mostly for the first few months, or even years, the man can be done well before he has learned to facilitate her satisfaction. A young couple might need some extra lubrication in the beginning. This would be our suggestion the night after the wedding. By the way, no matter how good or bad, nobody forgets their first time, and we wish more 'first times' could happen within a beautiful, strong, committed marriage relationship. Just as a general statement, if he loves her right and she responds, there is never bad sex.

Porn kills sex

There is a drive within the culture to normalize the porn industry. Porn stars are now being placed on platforms with rock stars and movie celebrities. They are being celebrated and brought mainstream. The result is the taboo of porn is being slowly purposely eroded by the multi-billion dollar industry. This is part of their strategy to drive it to every computer screen and into every unsuspecting heart.

> Porn kills. It is not worth it. Why invest in fake love when you can have the real thing.

But porn kills. It nearly destroyed our marriage. This is not the way a couple should 'spice' up their love life, as a leader once told me. This is the beginning of the end. Porn does many destructive things to mention a few:

- Porn dehumanizes women. Women become things that are merely there for the man's enjoyment. God did not create women as sexual objects. He created women in His image, to be honored and loved. She is designed to live within a sharing and loving community with her husband, as an equal partner.
- Porn has an addictive quality that leaves the addicted never satisfied. (A study found that sexuality specifically increases DeltaFosB in the nucleus accumbens, and plays a role as a mediator in natural reward memory. This study also found that overexpression of DeltaFosB induced a hypersexual syndrome.) This causes an escalating addiction that is never satisfied.
- Porn can cause less intimacy (Erectile Dysfunction) and depression. The American Psychological Association further cited a study from Brigham Young University and the University of Missouri finding men's use of porn associated with lower sexual quality for both men and their partners[1].

Virginity

If you are not a virgin:
- It is *not* ok because you have become 'one' with another. You will know what you are not supposed to know. It is like saying, taste this ice cream and now forget what it tastes like. You have already done something reserved for one person only.

> **If you are not a virgin, there is a solution.**

This 'one-time' intimacy is part of the glue God designed to hold couples together. Also, you can have the tendency to compare. Before, all you knew, was good. This does not even include all the pain and problems associated with breaking off with someone that you have slept with. It is like sticking duck tape together then trying to rip it apart. There can also be a marked difference between girls and boys in this area. Note the incongruence, boys sow their wild oats, but every boy wants a virgin on their wedding day. No real man wants used goods. For ladies, it is taboo and "slutty" to have multiple partners, although the hypocrisy is glaring.

> **Studs and sluts, neither are right!**

It is sad to note what drives young people to do this. Often the desire for *love, significance, and acceptance*. They end up having sex to find love and begin to erode their future love. This can cause an unhappy marriage eventually leading to divorce. Resulting in a broken family perpetuating the unfortunate cycle into the following generations. The emotional destruction needs to be noted. When a man takes advantage of a woman he does not feel good, like a man. He might have a brief sexual release but he soon realizes that he has *used* another human being. He has consumed her like an item. No man feels right about being a user. *He feels shame.* This might not present as such. You might find he cannot look at her quite the same or he might quickly break up with her. She now reminds him of his inadequacies. Conversely, she does not like to be used. Once they have been intimate, she feels like disposable goods, a dirty rag. Over time, she sees him and is reminded she was not worth waiting for or committing too. She feels used, and nobody likes to feel used.

- If you are *not* a virgin, it is ok, because God is full of grace! He can redeem and renew you. He can help you remove images and attitudes. He can help you stop comparing your beautiful spouse to all the past memories. He can turn any shame, fear and hurt into joy and confidence. He can make you new again.

> There is hope through Jesus Christ. You can be whole again.

Action: I suggest a time of prayer, fasting and celebration. It can be helpful to take the names and pictures of the 'past' and to burn them ceremonially. Lock in the commitment to this new union.

Then leave it! Leave it at the fire. Leave it at the Cross! Do not bring it up again. They are dead to you. Certainly, do not friend them on social media!

Making babies is fantastic fun
(when you are married and ready)

You now have a great excuse to have sex more often ... and all the boys cheer! And you have a reason to have sex at different times in the day ... and all the boys go wild! You have an excuse to try, and try and try and try again ... now the boys are hysterical!

> Making babies is fantastic. Enjoy each phase.

Rod's Unfortunate Story: I am not going to mention the time that I took a phone call in the middle of an intimate midday moment, or that I had to run out right away to meet a friend in crisis after a 'close' moment. By the way, we believe it was this exact moment that we can attribute to the conception of our beautiful third born. That friend, well, he will never know the incredible commitment and cost of that loving pastoral moment. Thanks Doug!

Now some people fall pregnant on the first attempt, and some take some time. But making babies is fun. Remember babies are a gift from God and each moment is to be savored. There is nothing more amazing than watching a woman grow into the incubator for this new life. Her very body and form is so beautiful. She will expand until she looks like she will explode! She will become uncomfortable towards the end and will be very tired. Love her. Care for her.

Talk to your new baby. There is much to be said about the interaction between parents and child/ren way before they are delivered. Enjoy each phase. You only get it once.

Some people will lose babies through no fault of their own, or even others! Some Moms will miscarry, placing enormous stress and sadness in their marriage. Treat every miscarriage as a young life lost and grieve appropriately. Check in with your doctor to discover some potential reasons. Miscarriages have been linked to divorce and suicide so please be aware of this and connect with a pastor or counselor immediately.

> **Losing a child puts tremendous pain and pressure on a marriage. Seek help!**

Cheryl Story: In our pre-marriage classes, we discussed having four children. We thought you decided on a number, did the 'deed' and there you have it! We, of course, knew everything about parenting, as we were youth group leaders, so naturally, we would bring up perfect kids!

It took a miscarriage, 18 months and a doctor to have our first bundle of joy. Our friends and family were shocked and understandably concerned at the news as, up until this point, we could not even keep the hardiest plants alive. We needed God's grace, love, and help!

When our firstborn was about a year and a half, I miscarried again. I, at this point, did not realize I was pregnant and Rod was away. It was early days, and life continued.

A little later we traveled to the USA with now a toddler and quickly fell pregnant. It was short-lived. I called the doctor, and then Rod, once I realized what was happening. He asked if he needed to leave his meeting and come home. I said I was fine, and that was the end of that.

We soon fell pregnant again. This time the doctor could hear two heartbeats, I was measuring bigger, and my blood work was indicating twins. I was excited, Rod was overwhelmed. At 16 weeks we lost one and delivered the undeveloped baby along with our stunning second born.

We were living in a foreign country with a kindergartner, a newborn and had had three miscarriages. I was now 31. Four bundles of joy was no longer an option.

Our girls grew up, Rod now 40, was really busy with the church, and I was consumed with the girls. He decided that we needed to 'try again.' I was not too enthusiastic, so went with our 'if it happens' plan. This had not worked before, so I was pretty sure I was 'safe.' I suddenly got really ill. Bunches of tests and many doctor visits later they announced my unexpected pregnancy. I was three months along. We told the girls, and announced to the church with first baby pics!

We now had a teenager and 'big girl' and soon a newborn to be added. Rod was 41 and felt he had missed out on the nurturing part of child rearing and this time he was going to be 'all in'! One night, the pregnant lady was hungry and cranky and wanted to go to McDonald's. Rod had a new 'no junk food' and no money for 'trash food' policy. After a rather loud 'conversation' we drove home in silence and 'food-less.' I quickly exited the car, threw on some mac and cheese, put the girls to bed, and got into bed in silence. The following day still mad, I went to my next doctor appointment, without Rod, as I felt he did not deserve to see our baby, he called, but I assured him 'I was fine!'

The nurse did her usual heartbeat checks and ultrasound. She called the doctor in, and they exchanged 'that look.' She wanted to know if anyone could meet me at the hospital as they needed 'better' equipment to check some things. My heart sank, and I called Rod, who flew there. As mad as I had been with him, there is no one else I wanted with me at that time. Our baby had died at 16 weeks. Rod begged to look one more time at the ultrasound, but it was too late.

Our doctor was terrific and very empathetic as he had journeyed the same journey as us. Six months later and with a lot of prayer and medication we were pregnant with Emlyn. Now at 40 and 42, we had our third beautiful little girl.

Going into marriage, we had so many ideals and knew everything about everything! We discovered we can do nothing without God, and even with Him right by our side things still don't always work out as we want, but we have Him with us to dry our tears and give us the strength to grow through the not so perfect parts of life. Marriage is similar in that it's not perfect, but it's better to go through the not so perfect parts of life with someone by your side.

Vasectomy

This is not fun, but I believe it is admirable that you, as the man, accept some responsibility for birth control. Plus a lot of female contraception's can hurt her. Plan this only when you are done building your family.

> **Very permanent contraception for guys!**

Some facts, it is painful but should take only a few days to recover. You will have no problems with an erection, and you will still copulate, only about half the seminal fluid will be ejected. Have the discussion with your lovely spouse before you do this, it *is* permanent!

What if you think you are gay

There is a lot of discussion about gender identity. Let me lean into the debate with just two points.

First: I believe that you are created by God as a gendered image bearer. That means that you are not just male physically but also spiritually. It is not something that can be changed with a snip and cut. It is who you are. If you are one of those folks that are wrestling with this, I would suggest before you abandon your gender, explore and enjoy all your gender has to offer. There are uniquely boy things and uniquely girl things. Dive into those. Enjoy them and celebrate what you are, not what you are not.

> **If you are a boy, enjoy all the amazing things of 'boyness', if you are a girl, rock all the great things about 'girlness'!**

Two: There is a time in a person's life when they hit puberty and become sexually aware. This sexual awareness can have many different results. It will certainly mean they change physiologically, but it will also bring change in how they think and how they feel. A boy can be among boys or a girl amongst girls and have some sexual feelings. This merely is sexuality coming alive and nothing else.

I have a fear that because of the current culture we are in, that this is misconstrued as being gay. Boys, for example, will get erections from very early in life but it is not connected to sex. It is merely for the pre-pubescent boy a fun trick that he can make his penis hard. At around puberty, he begins to become sexually aware. Combine growing numbers of broken homes, dysfunctional families, the lack of role-models, lousy sex education, internet porn, and sexual awareness, and you have all the ingredients for a society of feminized boys and masculine girls that have not had a fair opportunity to explore everything about being a boy and being a girl. This is sad and unfortunate.

Masturbation

Self-stimulation for sexual gratification has traditionally been a more male exercise, although there are growing statistics of females engaging in it. One of the main reasons, I believe, is boys become active in this from very early by merely 'playing' with their genitals. This will give them the sensation of sexual copulation, without the mature semen. The older a boy gets, he will then connect this stimulation to its sexual context. He will begin to ejaculate seminal fluid as his body and mind mature. For a boy, even the pressure of a safety belt on his pelvis, or a wash or shower, can bring on some of the same feelings. Naturally, a boy will typically have a morning erection, as a part of his body staying healthy, and that could

> Masturbation will not make you blind. But it will hurt your marriage.

include a nocturnal emission. This sets a young man up for exploring this stimulation further, and that often includes masturbation of some nature. Girls do not typically get the same natural sexual reactions when sleeping and bathing. Intimacy, for girls, is far more connected to the relationship aspect than the physical activities. This does not mean that girls cannot or do not self-stimulate, but it has a very different emotional connection for them.

Is it Ok? Is it biblical? What happens when we get married? I do not believe any scripture prevents this personal activity. There is one verse that some will refer to in Genesis 38:9

> *"But Onan knew that the child would not be his; so whenever he slept with his brother's wife, he spilled his semen on the ground to keep from providing offspring for his brother."*

God killed him for it! That sounds scary, but actually, God punished Onan because he did not fulfill his responsibility to provide a genetic line for his brother. This was not about the act of spilling sperm, this was about honoring God's instruction.

Another scripture in Leviticus 22:4[2] is interesting because here the priesthood family of Aaron is instructed they are not clean or pure if they touch someone who has an emission of semen. The scripture does not say, someone who has had intercourse or slept with a woman. So I would postulate that this person has either had a nocturnal emission or has masturbated.

> There are sexual responsibilities and family ones that God takes seriously.

Thereby we realize this activity was indeed happening. I do not find any Biblical grounds forbidding this activity, but before you send me an angry email, neither do I believe it is recommended or desirable, especially in a marriage. Sex is part of the glue keeping a married couple together. Sidestepping sex in marriage as a result of having been satisfied through self-stimulation is selfish and harmful to the union.

Masturbation is also not acceptable when conflict has caused some kind of rift between a couple. It is cowardly to gratify oneself instead of dealing with conflict and then enjoying mutually satisfying and unifying sex.

Often masturbation will be combined with sexual lusting or unhealthy fantasy, and we know that God is very clear about how wrong this is[3]. This really is the habit of boys and should not be a needed activity of real men. Real men (and women) enjoy growing in self-control and desire for the more significant activities of loving another human completely.

> **Masturbation can cause a lack of desire to pursue intimacy in your marriage.**

Mutual masturbation, oral sex and more

What does the Bible say? What is permitted? Scripture says in Hebrews 13:4

> *"Marriage should be honored by all, and the marriage bed kept pure, for God will judge the adulterer and all the sexually immoral."*

How do we keep the marriage bed pure? I believe we do this by keeping sex respectful and loving within the private partnership of the covenant community of the marriage and not allowing any external factor like pornography or lust for others into it. (Matthew 5:28).

But what about mutual stimulation, for the other person's sake? I believe that God is creative and made sex and intimacy something to be enjoyed and celebrated. So I believe that back rubs, soft music, mutual stimulation, kissing, oral intimacy, and the likes are all within the category of sexual pleasure within God's standards *when* the marriage partner is willing and enjoys the activity. 1 Corinthians 6:18 says:

> **Are you doing it out of love? Or is this driven by lust, porn or selfishness?**

"Flee from sexual immorality. All other sins a person commits are outside the body, but whoever sins sexually, sins against their own body."

Some criteria to consider:
- Are you wanting some of these sexual antics because it is a fantasy derived from R rated movies or porn? (not reality). Making someone behave or act anything less than a beautiful child of God cannot be sanctioned!

- Is this activity making him or her feel less or more? Is it degrading or dehumanizing or is it stimulating and encouraging? Remember we care more about the other person than ourselves in these activities. This is not a 'sort me out' session. If any of what you are doing hurts your spouse physically, mentally, spiritually or emotionally then it goes without saying that you need to stop! Take a note: Ephesians 5:25-28

"Husbands, love your wives, just as Christ loved the church and gave himself up for her to make her holy, cleansing her by the washing with water through the word, and to

present her to himself as a radiant church, without stain or wrinkle or any other blemish, but holy and blameless. In this same way, husbands ought to love their wives as their own bodies. He who loves his wife loves himself."

Shotgun weddings. (Oops, we're pregnant)

She is pregnant, and he wants to honor her and take responsibility. This sounds admirable on the front end, but I would ask you to pause and not make pregnancy the reason for a wedding. Can they work? Yes, of course, depending on the couple, but choosing to get married is vastly different from 'I guess I have to'. Both of you know this, and it will come back to affect you in the future.

Do not make one mistake become a lifetime of mistakes. There are many other options.

Abortion is not one of them!

> Sometimes we get the order mixed up. Do not follow a hiccup with more mistakes. Make a wise and Godly decision.

Contraception

I wade into complicated waters bringing this up. I do believe in the sanctity of life which begins with a fertilized egg. So any contraception that allows fertilization to happen and then destroys it by causing rejection or destruction is not good. Preventing ovulation, fertilization or copulation, I believe is ok. Birth control makes sense. God cares that your life and the life of your children is not so overwhelming that you cannot carry his light to your family and neighbors.

No Sex until you are married!

It is very simple, but hard to do. Just say 'no' for now for a lifetime of 'yes' in the future. Do not sacrifice on the altar of today what is a rewarding blessing for many years to come. God has an excellent plan for you and your intimacy and taking a Hollywood perspective will cause a Hollywood result.

God created sex and intimacy. Let's look at His perspectives, boundaries, and blessing on this crucial subject. Do you want great sex? Then do it God's way.

> **No sex until you are married! It's God's way, its the best way!**

ELEVEN C'S FOR A STRONG MARRIAGE

Speed Notes on Chapter 10

- Sex is fantastic, enjoy lots of it, when you are married, of course.
- Men, exercise self-control, you are not a rabbit! Help your ladies guard that alluring gift as it is designed for your marriage.
- Song of Solomon is a book in the bible that speaks about the beauty and process of loving a woman. This rather graphic literature is an inspiration that confirms that God is all for dynamic intimacy. When it is baby making time, have lots and lots of fun and make lots of babies!
- Past pains and inappropriate sexual experiences can significantly affect your sexual connection. Be open with each other and be aware of the potential pitfalls.
- Sex is about enjoying all of each other, not just the 'private parts'. Touch her heart, and you will get access to the rest of her. 'Hey, you awake?' is never a good intimacy starter. A loving professional will bring her to enjoyment as you maintain self-control.
- Men typically do not need to be encouraged to get naked but understand that women usually treat nakedness far differently. A woman's form is so much part of her self-esteem and confidence. Build that, and she will delight you. You see her naked, and you are instantly aroused, she sees you naked, and she wonders if you are cold.
- Porn kills love and treats women like trash. Porn will destroy your marriage and your

masculinity.
- God and only God, can and does restore those that have made bad decisions in the past.
- Masturbating will not make you blind, but could negatively affect your passion and desire for real intimacy. Be careful here. Mutual sexual arousal and creative sex needs to be discussed and must always be for the other person's benefit.
- If you are a boy, you are a boy, enjoy all the boy stuff. If you are a girl you are a girl, enjoy all the girl stuff. You are a God-created gendered image bearer.

NO SEX TILL YOU MARRIED!

Action Steps

- Stop having sex, or 'exciting love', until you are married.
- Stop doing porn.
- Do all the single boy and girls things you have wanted to do. Jump out of a plane, climb that mountain, go to that concert, island, adventure, because once you are married the union takes higher priority than your desires. This does not mean that fun stops or adventures disappear, they just become different, and the other person's desires become more important than your own. I find it strange, and devastating, that some live as single people trying to act married then get married and try to act single!
- Break free from past experience, go to counseling, go to confession, seek help. The least amount of 'past' you bring into your new marriage the better for you. This is not because you have failed, it is because you want the best for the future. Explore God's healing from sin and struggles.
- Begin reading the Bible together, it is a form of intimacy that few truly discover, and will feel strange and vulnerable in the beginning, but will develop into some of the most powerful moments of your life. Begin slowly and begin in the New Testament (the second half). I recommend 1 Corinthians.
- Exercise the spiritual discipline of *Solitude.*

CHAPTER 11

Celebration

The wedding is a once in a lifetime moment, take every second to savor it, live it, love it.

Chapter 11

Celebration

A Conversation about Faith and Fun

All this hard work. All the time, stress and resources invested in one momentous moment: the wedding! Is it worth it? Of course! This is the eleventh conversation.

The Wedding is a once in a lifetime moment that most girls dream about all their lives. It was my tangible expression of choosing, selecting and pursuing Cheryl and her considering and finding me worth it. It is like a real-life Disney movie.

> The Wedding is a once in a lifetime moment that most girls dream about all their lives.

Rod Story: When I facilitate a wedding celebration, I get the prime view as I look back down the aisle, with the groom. We stare down at the closed door, waiting, waiting. The music changes and the anticipation builds. And then she enters. It is always breathtaking. The groom almost always gets emotional as he sees his stunning bride enter and light up the room. She walks purposely and proudly toward her man.

He chose her, he wanted her, he cannot believe she said 'yes'. She is close now, and he can see the emotion in her face. She is radiant and overwhelmed, the emotions vacillating between extreme joy and tears. Can it be true that in a few minutes she will be his wife and he will be her husband? He cannot hear anything in the room. He tries to remember the rehearsal. He walks down to take her from her father's arm. Her Dad is slightly flustered. He remembers all the years in a flash. He cannot believe he is giving his princess away. They turn to me and the service begins. He says 'I do'. She says it too. This is the moment. This is the time. Here for the first time in his life, he takes his new wife. This is the first time she looks into her new husband's eyes. And they kiss.

It is moving, it is breathtaking, it is Divine. There is nothing like it! It touches the deepest level of us. It goes beyond the skin, beyond the mind, beyond the personality. It touches our souls!

Let us focus on what is important! Let us not get distracted by all the social media entrances to the latest pop tunes that seem to increase in stupidity. All these added elements tend to add stress, and stress is a wedding killer. What is supposed to be a celebration of love and commitment becomes a wrestle of the wills and in-laws.

> **Focus on what is important! This is your wedding and you should design it as you would like. Helpers are there to help.**

Wedding help

This is your wedding so no matter how willing and helpful 'others' are, you are not controlled or limited by their ideas or thoughts. It is ok to say no to a Mom or in-law. It is ok to reject a friend's thoughts.

Rod's Story: The only time I have ever said no to my mother in law was the night before our wedding. I wanted to be in the hall to decorate and was running late, I know you're shocked. Cheryl also wanted to come in, but as tradition has it, we are not supposed to see each other the night before. Needless to say, my lack of tack and my mother-in-law's insistence did not bid well, our first argument. We rebooted and have not fought since. She does bake a good pie so I would be silly to mess with that.

Setting the Date and the Engagement

Deciding on a date is entirely a personal decision, but do not take engagement lightly. An engagement can be a legally binding contract or promise of marriage. Do you notice the comments in the Bible when Joseph was engaged to Mary?[1]

> **Do not take engagement lightly. Do not abuse it.**

We do not favor an indefinite engagement period for a number of reasons:
- The widely held but dangerous belief that engagement entitles a couple to all the benefits of marriage.
- The longer you are engaged the more tempting it is to sleep with each other. We have spoken extensively about this throughout the book.
- Finally, you have exciting things to do and explore as a young married couple, why wait, let's get married!

Get your date out early so that people can plan to travel, if necessary, to share the important day with you. A frugal approach could utilize primarily online opportunities to communicate.

CELEBRATION

Preperation

Securing the pastor and engaging in pre-marital classes is *very important*. No matter how much 'experience' you have had with a member of the opposite sex you are heading to a place you have not been before. This is a foreign country and you need to learn and discover this new culture, language, and traditions. Do not be fooled into thinking that the latest reality show will give you enough information.

> **Pre-marital preparation is very paramount.**

Some characteristics you are looking for in the marriage pastor could include:
- personal relationship you have with or a Pastor you relate to (don't feel obliged to use any Pastor, for whatever reason)
- his or her time availability to show you an appropriate level of care and preparation and be available for follow-up.

Lock it in

In larger cities, banquet venues and churches can book up months and even years ahead. Do not be overwhelmed or disheartened by this. Just move one step forward each day. Securing these places will lock in your date and get the ball rolling. There is a growing trend for outdoor, destination or creative weddings. Some ideas are fantastic; some are horrendous - there are limits. Making something memorable, romantic and spiritual is fantastic, but we have seen some couples spoil the moment simply for the sake of unique-

> **Approach the tasks one at a time, this is no time to get overwhelmed.**

ness. There is only so much creativity you can employ in exchanging your vows. Let her be a princess, let him be a prince. This is not the time for the circus to come to town, keep it simple, yet special.

Rod's Story: Celebrations can have their stresses, but this one seemed to take the cake, literally. A young couple came to me to perform their wedding. They arrived at my church office and took a seat. The young man began talking about his vision for the wedding and we slid into a philosophical-theological conversation. It ended with him stating that he was excited for me to officiate at their marriage, and they handed me the date, time and place.

Just one little alternation, could I please not mention God. They felt unsure about the God thing and wanted me to instead use some handwritten vows that involved fairies. I said I would get back to them. I pondered for some time, prayed, and God gave me a great idea. I prepared a sermon all around the comment 'What if?' What if I knew something that would change your life, what if … I was excited and ready.

The day came, and I headed to the wedding venue. I was running a little closer to the start time than I had planned. So I rushed up to the door about 10 minutes before the service time to find it locked! I tried it again. At this point, I noticed no vehicles in the parking lot. I got on the phone and began calling contact numbers and friends. I discovered that the venue had in fact changed, and they now were at a local downtown pub. I rushed there concerned for the couple as they must all be waiting for me and they must be very concerned about my whereabouts and wellbeing.

I rushed into the back of the pub as I witnessed another 'pastor', I use that term lightly, ending a sentence about fairies and pronouncing them husband and wife.

They then had to walk straight down the centre of the pub, straight to where I was standing. Each slow and romantic step was made directly toward me. Once out the bar, the groom walked across to me and said he thought she had told me and she thought he had told me. They had decided to go with another pastor. Talk about weak masculinity.

I have heard of runaway brides and grooms but never a runaway wedding before.

The Week Before

The week before the wedding can be very hectic getting all the last things done. Remember to focus on the main things, delegate to the entourage and find time to breathe. This is a celebration but it has all the ingredients of a production. As with all productions, there are certain things that cannot be done until it is 'go time'. This will have inherent stress so try to enjoy the adventure and know that it will be all right. Be nice to each other and others.

> **Delegate, laugh, accept what cannot be done and be nice to each other.**

The Night Before

The night before can be a very special evening. Most pastors will have a rehearsal. This is the last chance to go through the line-up and the order of service. Checking all technology would be greatly encouraged.

Then the team could head to a rehearsal dinner together. This is a perfect (real, intimate and un staged) occasion for parents to speak into the lives of their children, on their last night as singles. This is also the time for in-laws to bond into a new extended family.

Imagine if instead of silliness or "bachelor" or "bachelorette" stuff, the night before is used in a powerful way. How about a group of men gathering to call out, in the man, some of the characteristics that they see in him? Those that make him capable for the task of being a husband and father. He could receive the family crest as a sign of the passing on of the baton, the family name, and heritage. How would this young man and son feel?

> This could be the most powerful night in a young couples wedding preparation. Do not miss the opportunity with frivolity.

What could it look like if a group of ladies recognized in the bride all the traits of a blessed woman? Can you picture the tears and laughter and hugs and hollering as the people gathered around these two. They now begin the story of their new lives together. Chapter One! They could end the night in prayer for the next day. Radical we know - but far more impacting, life-changing and powerful than any another dinner that ends in beer pong.

The Day

The day itself will begin far earlier for the ladies than the men. A light breakfast and they are off to hair appointments, nails, dresses, makeup and more. They will collect flowers, and any other supplies needed for the day and head to the church. They will typically do their final dressing at the Church.

Most Churches will secure a 'green room', a changing and preparation area for the bride and her team. This is typically secured from the groom, so he does not see her before she enters the church. We highly recommend that. Some photographers will try to get pictures of the couple before the service in a new trend called the 'private reveal'. We would encourage you not to do that. It spoils something extraordinary, the great entrance, the wow,

The men will grab a lengthy breakfast at the local pancake shop and, typically, load up on the bacon. They will then typically pick up a golf game or something and head to the shower then get dressed. Most men arrive dressed at the church. They will usually hang around and welcome guests as they come. They will have one of the ladies help them pin on the corsages, the get ready for line-up.

Wedding Time

Breath! Everybody is ready, and it is time to start.

You will want to get lined up. We like to ask the Grandparents to lead the procession. This is a sign of respect for the previous generation and gives them a part of this fantastic day. Then we get the bride's Mom to enter with the groom's parents. They will light the unity candle, or present sand art or any other visuals used in the celebration.

It is here!
Stop!
Breath!
Enjoy!

Story: We included communion and worship in our service. This was special and important to us as we wanted to make a statement about our Christian faith. As youth group and active leaders in the church, casting a good vision was essential to us. The day was overwhelming and very emotional, and I can remember greeting my ministry mentor, Mr. Dave, who had just had a stroke. In the emotive state of the moment I gave him a big kiss on the cheek by mistake, something certainly not typical in our culture and a huge surprise to both myself and Mr. Dave. It was sort of like saying "I love you" on a voice mail to your boss when unintended. I know you have done that too!

The Conclusion

At the conclusion of the service, the bride and groom will lead out on each other's arm. The entourage will follow.

We encourage the couple to have a master of ceremonies explain what is happening next. Typically it would be something like this:

> 'The lovely couple will be heading to have pictures taken, feel free to go to the reception. There are extra maps at the front door if you did not bring yours from your invitation. Once you get there, there will be some cheese and crackers and light refreshments. There is a seating chart as you enter, please find your table and enjoy some conversation until the happy couple arrives. When they arrive, we will open the bar that will serve beer, wine, and champagne and then serve a lovely dinner. The DJ will guide you once you get there.'

Budget

Focus on what is key. Concluding your special day being thousands of dollars in debt is not the wisest way to begin your new life together. Remember financial pressure is the number one cause of divorce, after communication.

> **Plan to spend 5-10% more than you thought, because surprises happen.**

There are some further practical resources in Chapter 13.[2]

CELEBRATION

Speed Notes on Chapter 11

- It's a very, very special day, a once in a lifetime day, do not mess it up by making it about you. This is your first chance to really make it about loving another person.
- Enjoy each moment of the preparation and planning of this special day. It shouldn't be all on the Bride.
- Step up, do not let your parents, friends or helpers bully either of you into things that you does not want.
- Be a guardian of the growing costs. No, not a Scrooge, but a guide.
- Be romantic when you propose, 'Hey we might as well get married, you want this?' will not make her feel chosen and treasured. Think about it, plan it, get excited about it, and enlist the help of friends and total strangers. Make it memorable. Then post it!
- In your role as spiritual leader, encourage great commitment to pre-marriage classes, a good class is well worth it.
- The night before can be very special, spend some time talking about what this can look like. This can be very different than flirting, feasting and falling down. P.S. Chest flasks are not good groom gifts.
- Be early for your wedding day and you do not need 'anything' to calm the nerves. This is your moment.
- Stop! Breath! Enjoy!
- It does not matter, whatever little things got missed, whatever someone said under stress,

whatever choices were made, nothing matters at this point. The only thing we need is a bride, a groom, a commitment, God and a Pastor. All the rest is just decoration.

Action Steps

- Build a wedding budget together. Be frugal and then add 5-10% for overages.
- Have an open meeting with the parents and explain to them your vision. Tell them how much you love them, but it is your wedding. Help them understand that you will take all their thoughts and ideas into consideration. At the end of the day it will be what the two of you dream about for your wedding.
- Work your way down the task list. Give yourself enough time, but also we would encourage you to not be engaged for more than 2 years in total. That is about the time self-control totally collapses and you land in no man's land relationally.
- Exercise the spiritual discipline of *Celebration.*

CHAPTER 12

Conclusion

*This is a journey not a destination.
It will take a lifetime to master.*

Chapter 12

Conclusion

Now What?

What you put in you get out!

The reason for writing this book is to give every person a fighting chance at having a strong marriage. We chose those words purposely. You will have to fight for it!

Rod's Story: For me, it began with a gun, a girl and a gurney. The young man was about seventeen years old. I heard the calamity in the ER before he even got to us. 'There's been a shooting, there's been a shooting!' Moments later, a young person was rushed into ER 1. My immediate observation was the expensive clothes he had on. There was virtually no blood, except a bit on his face. In auto mode, I began cutting off his designer wear, something we did with every person in an emergency situation.

> **This is a journey not a destination. It will take a lifetime to master.**

I heard in the background conversation about the arrival of the boy's parents and girlfriend. There were tears and screams from the waiting room.

Throughout the rest of that night, I would hear the details of the story emerge. This young man, had expensive clothing, a family that cared, a loving girlfriend, and a waiting room full of friends. However, he still took a handgun and placed it purposefully against his temple and pulled the trigger. He sort of messed this up as he shot through

CONCLUSION

his anterior fontanelle. This did not cause him to die. It would take an additional 12 hours before the shock wave of the bullet would slowly erode into the soft tissue of the rest of his brain and finally, at about 8am the next morning, would cause him to flatline.

That was the moment for me! That was the time that I realized everything that Charles from the Green House Bible Study group had said. That was the first time all my Church past and Cheryl's comments made sense. That was the moment when real faith took hold of me. I saw hopelessness in the face of prosperity, popularity and present parenting. I saw a young man who had it all. A young man who had what I wanted, yet he chose to end it all.

As the EKG alarm sounded and the Doctor pronounced his passing, at that moment, in tears, I said yes to Jesus. Yes to a God who loves me, yes to a Lord who formed me, yes to a Savior who died for me. That changed my life forever.

We dream throughout this book, you have lived, learned and grown closer to God and your best friend. We hope it does not take a death for Jesus Christ to be a reality for you. We hope this book has helped, we hope your marriage journey will concretize your faith and empower you to impact others.

> We dream throughout this book, you have lived, learned and grown closer to God and your best friend.

This is just the vision document. This is not the end, but the beginning. Now is the time to put this all into practice. There will be times when you will have to return to the notes and get clarity again. Sometimes you might relook at your own comments in the discussion questions. But never stop persevering, never stop growing, and maturing in faith and in your marriage. Remember the cake from the beginning of the book? What you put in is what you get out.

Some practical routines that will help:

Have a Weekly Date

Try making this a part of the DNA of your family. Making your husband or wife a weekly priority will head off many challenges in the future. If you think about how many hours you spend at work, continued education, household chores, remodeling, sports, recreation, friends and eventually children, no wonder our marriages suffer. These are all important, but we need to keep the main thing the main thing. Loving God and loving our spouse. You look after your relationship, and you will be surprised how much the two of you will achieve together. We find it so sad when a couple conquers the business world, the social world, even the spiritual world but loses their marriage in the process.

Have an Annual Marriage Retreat

You can choose to go on a teaching and training weekend or rest back with a good marriage book on the beachfront that you both read. But, if once a year, you facilitate a significant input into your marriage, you will reap incredible richness from it.

> And the two will become one.

CONCLUSION

No TV in the Bedroom

That is for sleeping, praying, and sex. Ending the day with garbage news or a good conversation is your choice, we recommend the later.

Meeting

Plan Sunday night to include an administration meeting, not too romantic, but very important. Begin each week with your schedules and the budget and make sure you are continuously on the same page. A cup of coffee and some conversation will launch your week off well.

Go Offline

Communication and digital tools should be put to bed at least an hour before you call it a night. Unless you are a doctor or a first responder, there is no real reason to be online 24/7. This will enable you to detox from the day and refocus your attention on those you love. We even suggest a change of clothes when you get home. It will change your mindset.

Leave Work at Work

Do not bring work home. Each person is different. Some will need a workout some will need a nap, some will just have to pull over and breath in the driveway. But leave your work at work so that your home is indeed a sanctuary.

Pray Together

Pray daily with each other, it is a beautiful intimacy

that will draw you closer to God and each other. A quiet time at the beginning or end of your day, filled with prayer and scripture will reboot your thinking and refocus your love daily.

Have Regular Sex

Have sex and lots of it. Yes, you can. Once you're married, have plenty of romantic, passionate, intimate mutually satisfying sex. Boys fight way less when their ladies are naked. Just saying!

Stay Together

Stick it out! Do not give up. You can truly enjoy the oneness that you read about in Scripture. This is a rich and rewarding place that few find. Beat the odds and finish the race. This is not referring to cases of abuse or where your life or the life of your children is at risk. Here, seek help immediately.

Have Regular Adventures

Do not allow life to become dull and humdrum. Live a little, laugh a little, because you will move through the phases of life so much more quickly than you can imagine. You think you will be in your 20's forever and suddenly you are having your 50th birthday. Take opportunities in each life phase to enjoy it to the maximum. When you're single be incredibly single, when you're married be passionately married, when you have young kids be phenomenal parents. When you have older kids be the cool Dad and Mom, ok, too far, you will never be cool, remember your parents? Then when you are silver and wise enjoy

CONCLUSION

each other as best friends, seasoned lovers, and spiritual giants. Love God and love each other until death parts you. The reality is it will come sooner than you think, but you will not believe me now, and that's ok.

Move

If you read this book because you're having troubles, keep on keeping on. Do not stop. Keep fighting *for* each other, not with each other. If you read this because he does not care or she has gone cold, pray hard and faithfully. Ask and trust God for a breakthrough, reach out for help. Ask God to please change *you*! If you are reading this because you want a strong marriage, be encouraged. Those that prepare well are more likely to succeed. Continue growing into the 'kind of person the person you are looking for is looking for.' [1]

> If your marriage is in trouble, keep on working on it. If he does not care and she is cold, reach out for help and keep praying. If you want a strong marriage, be encouraged, those that prepare well are far more likely to succeed.

Keep Learning

Never stop discovering more! More about each other and more about marriage. Read, listen, learn and love. Marriage is a great adventure. Enjoy!

Let us conclude with a prayer:

> *Dear Lord, thank you. Thank you for your powerful and dynamic vision of marriage. The idea of bringing a man*

and a woman together in this divine union. The beauty of first loves, the wonder of the adventure, the power of intimacy. Lord, only you could have made something so personal, so enjoyable and yet also so valuable. The miracle of self and other discovery in this safe and secure incubator of life. Thank you.

Lord, we take a moment to raise up the person or people reading this book. We ask you to be gracious in their lives. We pray that they stay the course, that they resist the evil one as he intends to destroy their beautiful union. We ask you to please give them the desire to complete the action steps and to continue to pursue your best. Please help them Lord to never be satisfied with a mediocre marriage but to strive to grow into the people that are continuously transforming more into Your likeness. Help them unpack their faith in the community of a loving marriage. Help them to take that understanding and maturing into their families and into the world around them.

We take a moment, Lord, to cover in prayer those reading this because life or their marriage is tough right now. We know something that represents Your very personality and reflects Your face will be targeted, will be attacked. We pray for strength for these people, we pray for peace for these warriors, we pray for tenacity and determination for these lovely people. I ask you, Lord, to give them breakthrough, power, and perseverance.

Lord, we conclude by giving you all the glory for the marriages resurrected and lives changed through this journey that you have taken us on. Jesus, we thank you for your grace and the gift of eternal life. We live for You, and live our lives outwards towards others. May our marriages represent you well. Amen.

CONCLUSION

Speed Notes on Chapter 12

- This is a journey, not a destination. It will take a lifetime to master.
- Have a weekly date.
- Plan an annual marriage retreat.
- No TV in the bedroom.
- Have a weekly planning meeting, you should initiate this.
- Choose technology-free times or days. Get offline, and you will 'get on' better.
- Leave work at work.
- Plan adventures, make life interesting, succeeding at work might hold your interest, but she fell in love with you. Take opportunities to enjoy each other. This can so easily fade quickly after the wedding.
- Stay together, use your masculine strength and determination to win. Don't turn into a self-consumed boy that pouts and wines when he is struggling.
- Keep moving, never be satisfied with where you have gotten because there is always where you can be. Movement is oxygen to men. Breathe deeply.
- Become a spiritual leader in your family, pray with your lovely lady.

Action Steps

- Lock in your schedule for your meetings and the annual retreat
- Lovers who know **God's love** are more magnificent lovers, it's easy to give when

you have significantly received.
- Switch off technology and enjoy each other.
- Six months after your wedding, send your spouse the letter you wrote in Chapter 1.

CHAPTER 13

Contributions

Chapter 13

Contributions

Bibliography

Foreword

<1>   https://www.inkanyezi.co.za/

Introduction

<1>   https://en.wikipedia.org/wiki/Pictionary

Chapter 1

<1>   Genesis 1:27 "So God created mankind in his own image, in the image of God he created them; male and female he created them."

Chapter 2

<1>   "What else does this craving, and this helplessness, proclaim but that there was once in man a true happiness, of which all that now remains is the empty print and trace? This he tries in vain to fill with everything around him, seeking in things that are not there the help he cannot find in those that are, though none can help, since this infinite abyss can be filled only with an infinite and immutable

object; in other words by God himself." - Blaise Pascal, Pensées VII(425)

<2> http://www.mayoclinic.org/diseases-conditions/narcissistic-personality-disorder/basics/definition/con-20025568

Chapter 3

<1> http://www.5lovelanguages.com/

<2> https://markgungor.com/

Chapter 4

<1> Saving Your Marriage Before It Starts by Les Parrott, Leslie Parrott

<2> https://www.theguardian.com/lifeandstyle/2007/jun/09/familyandrelationships

Chapter 5

<1> King James Version Translation

<2> James 1: 3-4 'The testing of your faith produces perseverance. Let perseverance finish its work so that you may be mature and complete, not lacking anything.'

<3> 1 Corinthians 13:11 "When I was a child, I talked like a child, I thought like a child, I reasoned like a child. When I became a man, I put the ways of childhood behind me."

<4> https://markgungor.com/

<5> https://www.daveramsey.com

Chapter 6

<1> Acts 18:22 'After removing Saul, he made David their king. God testified concerning him: 'I have found David son of Jesse, a man after my own heart; he will do everything I want him to do.''

<2> Mark 12:30 'Love the Lord your God with all your heart and with all your soul and with all your mind and with all your strength.'

<3> Mark 12:31 'The second is this: 'Love your neighbor as yourself.' There is no commandment greater than these.''

<4> Genesis 1-2

<5> A Million Dream https://www.youtube.com/watch?v=pSQk-4fddDI

<6> https://www.geocaching.com/play

Chapter 7

<1> Maternal inheritance also gave rise to the idea that there exists a "Mitochondrial Eve," a woman from whom all living humans inherited their mitochondrial DNA. (https://www.nytimes.com/2016/06/24/science/mitochondrial-dna-mothers.html?_r=0)

CONTRIBUTIONS

<2>   Andy Stanley - https://andystanley.com/

<3>   Matthew 19:7-9 "Why then," they asked, "did Moses command that a man give his wife a certificate of divorce and send her away?" Jesus replied, "Moses permitted you to divorce your wives because your hearts were hard. But it was not this way from the beginning. I tell you that anyone who divorces his wife, except for sexual immorality, and marries another woman commits adultery.'"

<4>   1 Corinthians 7:15-17 'But if the unbeliever leaves, let it be so. The brother or the sister is not bound in such circumstances; God has called us to live in peace. How do you know, wife, whether you will save your husband? Or, how do you know, husband, whether you will save your wife? Nevertheless, each person should live as a believer in whatever situation the Lord has assigned to them, just as God has called them. This is the rule I lay down in all the churches.'

<5>   Doug Higgins

<6>   A Few Good Men

<7>   Ron Sanderson-Smith

<8>   https://www.aarp.org/caregiving/financial-legal/free-printable-advance-directives/

Chapter 8

Chapter 9

<1> http://www.usatoday.com/story/money/personalfinance/2016/10/12/average-credit-card-debt/91431058/

<2> https://www.daveramsey.com/budgeting/how-to-budget/

<3> https://www.crownmoneymap.org/MoneyMap/ASP/budgetguide.asp

<4> https://www.psychologytoday.com/blog/high-octane-women/201203/why-mess-causes-stress-8-reasons-8-remedies

<5> James 4:13-14 'Now listen, you who say, "Today or tomorrow we will go to this or that city, spend a year there, carry on business and make money." Why, you do not even know what will happen tomorrow. What is your life? You are a mist that appears for a little while and then vanishes.'

<6> Malachi 3:10 'Bring the whole tithe into the storehouse, that there may be food in my house. Test me in this," says the Lord Almighty, "and see if I will not throw open the floodgates of heaven and pour out so much blessing that there will not be room enough to store it.'

<7> https://www.daveramsey.com/blog/how-teens-can-become-millionaires

Chapter 10

CONTRIBUTIONS

<1> https://www.medicaldaily.com/you-think-you-know-erectile-dysfunction-you-dont-8-little-known-causes-impotence-310222

<2> Leviticus 22:4 "'If a descendant of Aaron has a defiling skin disease[a] or a bodily discharge, he may not eat the sacred offerings until he is cleansed. He will also be unclean if he touches something defiled by a corpse or by anyone who has an emission of semen,"

<3> Matthew 5:27-28 "'You have heard that it was said, 'You shall not commit adultery.' But I tell you that anyone who looks at a woman lustfully has already committed adultery with her in his heart.'

Chapter 11

<1> Matthew 1:18-19 'This is how the birth of Jesus the Messiah came about: His mother Mary was pledged to be married to Joseph, but before they came together, she was found to be pregnant through the Holy Spirit. Because Joseph her husband was faithful to the law, and yet did not want to expose her to public disgrace, he had in mind to divorce her quietly.'

<2> ### *Wedding Resources*

Invitations

Who to invite is also a tough conversation. Between his friends, her friends, Dad's office friends and Mom's book club you are clipping that 300-400 level before you realize it. You can be very focused here. Biological family on both sides and a close friend or two. The rest will get over it. After all, if they really care about you they will understand.

Payment

Who will pay for the wedding is another challenge. Tradition says the girl's family picks up most of the expenses. However, it has become more common for both families and even the bridal couple to chip in. With a healthy and sensible budget and good mature family relationships, this conversation can feel more like vision casting and be exciting rather than limiting and fragmenting. Frugal decisions here will pave the way for other lavish investments in your future, like the honeymoon, transportation, accommodation, education and more.

Rings

It starts here. The man traditionally purchases an engagement ring and wedding ring. When he proposes - and she accepts - he places the engagement band on her wedding finger (the finger, next to the pinkie on the left hand). At the actual wedding ceremony the couple exchange rings. She gets another and he gets his first. Keep it simple, make it elegant.

Cheryl's Story: Make sure it is real. We went to London to visit the queen, well actually we took a mission team and stayed on after the trip. It was quite the experience. The old inner city streets are filled with musicians, artists and buskers. We enjoyed the beat and rhythm of the culture. One of the things you will find on the highways and byways are people who try to sell you 'treasures.' We were warned that most of these are tricks and cons and one should stay away. I ended up speaking to this nice lad, and before long he was telling me that he had real gold jewelry for record low prices. He even offered to take it into the local jeweler for evaluation and verification. Rod shared his hesitations and concern. After some quick talking, I left with treasures and lighter by $50. We continued to travel, and towards the end of the trip, we had to rush to catch a ferry. It was only on this hectic run that I noticed Rod's shirt changing color. The gold from the 'real bling' was changing his shirt to a dirty dark gold yellow as the gold spray paint flowed from the rusty chain onto my souvenir t-shirt. With hearts beating and adrenaline flowing we sat on the boat laughing at the fake 'treasures' and our gullible attitudes. Rod remind me that he was right and that my ring unlike his bling was in fact real!

Stationery
Thank-you cards and other printing or digital media need consideration also.

Entourage
Remember it is perfectly fine to have just a best man and a maid of honor. Having twenty people up front is certainly not needed, no matter how pretty it looks. A flower girl and a page can be an entertaining addition but again are not needed, keep it simple. Although we had 12 bouncing youth group kids in ours, as you can see we have matured some.

Dresses and Suits
With a clear picture in your mind, you can em-

power your 'best man and maid of honor' to help you secure these. Are you going to rent or buy? Are you going to let the en- tourage choose or are you going to dictate? Are you having dresses made? If these questions begin to get overwhelming, keep it simple. We believe the new tradition 'Say yes to the dress!" might be fun but is not needed.

Photographer/Video
You will want to move on the photographer and/or videographer early as good professionals are booked well in advance.

Story: Our photographer was a lovely person but choose to shoot outdoors, at night, with little light. The men were all dressed in black. Picture floating ghostlike faces, white teeth in a sea of darkness surrounding a beautiful white dress. Our wedding album got stranger and slightly eerie the later in the evening it got.

Browse through your friends pictures, check online, and observe social media for examples that will assist you to choose the right style for you. You can already think of that one wedding with those magazine looking shots, book them!

DJ/Music
The DJ and music need to be selected for both the celebration and the reception. We would suggest negotiating with the DJ to handle both. This way there are no added costs. One really needs some amplification for the celebration service because often the bride and groom do not speak up due to nerves, or emotions. Three or four well-chosen songs are

needed, they need to be appropriate for weddings.

Catering

Food: Our suggestion is to keep it simple. Two types of meat are plenty, two vegetables and some salad and you are set. Dessert can really be the wedding cake. It is tradition to keep the top layer for the one year anniversary but this can present some practical challenges. Make the rest cupcakes for easy serving. They can be appropriately decorated.

Drink: We do not like to see the wedding couple getting drowned in alcohol on the big day. Getting to the reception well- oiled and lasting 50% of your special night is, in our opinion, a crass waste of money and a failure on the part of the 'best man and bridesmaid. You can drink anytime, but you cannot enjoy this day again. This also goes for the guests. We are flabbergasted at how much couples spend on this line item at weddings. You do not need to have an open bar. What we suggest is water, pop/soda/coke while the guests wait for the happy couple to get pictures done. It is not your responsibility to keep crazy uncle John lubricated until you return some 45 minutes to an hour later. Depending on your faith and spiritual understanding, when you arrive we suggest that you open up beer, wine, and champagne. These will be used for the toasts and for the social drinkers. We would not offer hard liquor at any stage. It is too expensive and could cause some issues later in the night.

Florist

Flowers and greenery can sneak up on you. You will

want to secure a price and timing. The bride is the main concern. Having some boutonnieres for the men and other selected special people is appropriate. Sometimes there are added arrangements for the Church altar, the pews or chairs and the main table at the reception. These can be pricey so keep it discreet. People come for the couple, not the decor.

Transportation

How are you getting there and back? Honestly, we think this is the least important of the whole ceremony. It is nice to have 3 pink stretch limousine but nobody remembers what you drove in any way, except if it really was three pink stretch limos! As long as they are clean, safe, and driven by someone responsible and respectable, you will have a wonderful time. Now a big yellow school bus might be remembered, but not what we looking for.

Multimedia/Specials

Some couples create powerpoint or entry dances. These can be worked on once the structure is finalized. A few classes at your local ballroom studio is recommended. The is nothing more beautiful than a father-daughter Viennese waltz, with her flowing dress and her tearful Dad.

Budget Example

Below is a rough example based on average spending in the USA of expense allocation of total budget:

Ceremony Total (33%)
- Venue (2%)
- Officiant (2%)

CONTRIBUTIONS

- Decor/Flowers (7%)
- Attire (10%) - Rings (12%)

Reception Total (62%)
- Food x 250 guests (36%)
- Drinks x 250 guests (13%)
- Music/DJ (3%)
- Video/Camera (10%)

Other Total (5%)
- Stationery (2.5%)
- Transportation (2.5%)

The Night Before

Most pastors will have a rehearsal. This gets all the team on the same page. It is typically 45 minutes to 1 hour. We would encourage you to be a little early so as to get organized. If you are planning to decorate the Church, this could be a time to do that. Some couples will arrive a few hours early and set up for the following day. This is the last chance to go through the line-up and the order of service. Checking all technology would be greatly encouraged. We suggest new batteries in all equipment.

Wedding Time

There are a few ways to line up the rest of the people standing up:
- One: Boys go in first and when the music starts they stand up and look back towards the door.
- Two: The boys go in followed by the girls and the bride.
- Three: The boys and girls go in together on each other's arm. The last lady in the procession, be-

fore the bride, is the Maid of Honor or Bridesmaid. She needs to check the bride so she is 100% ready before she enters. The page and flower girl typically will come in just before the bride. They will sprinkle flower petals. It is best that they stand right in front of the maid of honor and the best man when they get to the altar/stage. Small kids can be relocated to parents in the front row. The music changes and the congregation rises. The bride comes in on her Father's left arm (typically the groom's family sits on stage left and the bride's family stage right - that is looking from the stage towards the guests). The service continues from here.

The Conclusion

At the end of the service, the married couple can leave in a few different ways:
- One - The entourage lines up in a receiving line so the whole congregation can greet them,
- Two - The couple returns into the church and releases the congregation one row at a time, visiting and greeting the people as they leave.
- Three - The couple leaves for photographs and visits with the guests at the reception - a recommended way.

Chapter 12

<1> A term made popular by preacher and teacher Andy Stanley from North Point Ministries (northpoint.org)

CHAPTER 14

Acknowledgements

Chapter 14

Acknowledgements

Contributing Community

We wish to thank the many people who made this project of passion possible:

Firstly, our most profound and greatest thanks go to our parents, Ronald and Brenda Sanderson-Smith and Harry and Veronica Caine for showing us what marriage can look like. Their commitment to each other and to their families weaves all the way throughout this book.

Thank you to our families for their support and encouragement with this adventure, Michael Sanderson-Smith, and Janine Lee. And a special thanks to Robert Caine for the inspiration, motivation, and many late night conversations.

Thank you also to Deon Engelke, Krystal Moralee, Mark and Sue Delong, and my Dad, Ron Sanderson-Smith, for their hard work and editing.

Thank you to the man who changed our lives, Charles from the Green House Bible study, and my friend Ray Dauberman who has been a lifelong friend.

Thank you to friends and family who proofread and gave input on the text, Ron Rickard, Bob Lawson, Aaron Burrell, Bob Gresh, Craig Ayers, Linda Prendergast and Mark Williams.

ACKNOWLEDGEMENTS

Thank you to the many pastors and leaders that we have sat under that have influenced this material, especially Steve Andrews, Dave Wilson and Derrick Jolliffe.

Thank you to the many, many students who have traveled through our classes over the years, and who have helped shape this book.

Finally, thanks, of course, to God for His grace and favor in our lives. For His leading, His words, His inspiration, and His great idea, the idea of marriage.

You, the reader, can be a further part of this adventure in three more ways:

1) You can pick up the Workbook,
Eleven C's for a Strong Marriage Workbook

2) You can connect through our website,
https://Elevencsforastrongmarriage.com

3) If you have any comments,
please email us at
Elevencsforastrongmarriage@gmail.com.

www.ingramcontent.com/pod-product-compliance
Lightning Source LLC
LaVergne TN
LVHW051544070426
835507LV00021B/2404